CW01163062

# WOODWORKING PROJECTS

35 DIY WOOD PROJECTS FOR BEGINNERS AND
ADVANCE. A COMPLETE STEP-BY-STEP GUIDE
WITH INDOOR AND OUTDOOR PLANS.
INCLUDES INSTRUCTIONS, PHOTOGRAPHS
AND DIAGRAMS EASY TO FOLLOW

TOM FOSTER

© Copyright 2020 - All rights reserved.

The content contained within this book may not be reproduced, duplicated or transmitted without direct written permission from the author or the publisher.

Under no circumstances will any blame or legal responsibility be held against the publisher, or author, for any damages, reparation, or monetary loss due to the information contained within this book. Either directly or indirectly.

Legal Notice:

This book is copyright protected. This book is only for personal use. You cannot amend, distribute, sell, use, quote or paraphrase any part, or the content within this book, without the consent of the author or publisher.

Disclaimer Notice:

Please note the information contained within this document is for educational and entertainment purposes only. All effort has been executed to present accurate, up to date, and reliable, complete information. No warranties of any kind are declared or implied. Readers acknowledge that the author is not engaging in the rendering of legal, financial, medical or professional advice. The content within this book has been derived from various sources. Please consult a licensed professional before attempting any techniques outlined in this book.

By reading this document, the reader agrees that under no circumstances is the author responsible for any losses, direct or indirect, which are incurred as a result of the use of information contained within this document, including, but not limited to, — errors, omissions, or inaccuracies.

# TABLE OF CONTENT

| | |
|---|---|
| **INTRODUCTION** | 5 |
| **SIMPLE PLANS FOR BEGINNERS** | 10 |
|     1. Living Room Box | 10 |
|     2. Hinged Box | 11 |
|     3. Wooden Chopping Board | 13 |
|     4. Mirror Frame | 14 |
|     5. Wine Rack | 15 |
| **SHELVES (BEGINNERS PLAN)** | 17 |
|     1. Floating Shelves | 17 |
|     2. Honeycomb Shelves | 18 |
|     3. Leather Strap Shelf | 20 |
|     4. Woodwork Plan for a Basic Bookshelf | 21 |
| **BENCHES, CHAIRS AND STOOLS (INTERMEDIATE PLAN)** | 23 |
|     1. Work Bench | 23 |
|     2. Three-Legged Stool | 24 |
|     3. Simple Chair | 25 |
| **WOODWORKING PROJECTS FOR KITCHEN (ADVANCE PLAN)** | 28 |
|     1. Under sink storage: | 28 |
|     2. Hanging Pot Rack | 32 |
| **BEDS (ADVANCE PLAN)** | 37 |
|     1. Queen Slat Bed | 37 |
| **INNOVATIVE CREATIONS** | 41 |
|     1. Mini Desk Masterpiece | 41 |
|     2. Rustic Pallet Wagon | 41 |
|     3. Quirky Office Desk | 43 |
|     4. Practical Pallet Chair | 44 |
|     5. Super Slim End Table | 45 |
| **SMALL FURNITURE (BEGINNERS PLAN)** | 46 |
|     1. Bathroom Shelf Unit | 46 |
|     2. Handy Box | 52 |

## GARDEN FURNITURE WITH WOOD PALLETS (BEGINNERS PLAN) — 60
- 1. Pallet Garden Sofa — 60
- 2. Shelves for Garden — 61
- 3. DIY Garden Chair — 62
- 4. DIY Coffee Table — 63
- 5. Pallet Stool for Garden — 64

## PLANTERS; SHEDS; AND PLAYHOUSE (BEGINNERS PLAN) — 66
- 1. Playhouse in Patio — 66
- 2. Rack to Keep Your Tools — 67
- 3. Pallet Bin for Compost and Plants — 68
- 4. Grow Your Herbal Garden — 69
- 5. Storage Shed for Garden — 70

## GARDEN BENCH AND CHAIRS (INTERMEDIATE PLAN) — 72
- 1. Garden Bench — 72
- 2. Camp Kitchen — 74
- 3. Adirondack Chair — 77

## "MARSH FOX" DUCK PUNT (ADVANCE PLAN) — 88

## OUTDOOR DECK (ADVANCE PLAN) — 96

## CONCLUSION — 103

# INTRODUCTION

Woodworking has seen an increase in popularity over the past few years. In the past, woodworking which is actually a part of carpentry, was a norm. People built their own houses, patios, tables, furniture, etc. However, with modernization, now most of us just buy our furniture from IKEA or some other store.

Woodworking is catching on these days among thousands of enthusiasts because people are realizing that it is a cool way to be creative and there is a certain sense of pride and fulfilment that comes about from seeing something you have created that is beautiful and useful.

There is no end to what you can build if you have a good grasp of the fundamentals of woodworking. You could build sheds, chicken coops, garages and so much more.

What is most important is that you have the basic skills to work with the wood safely and efficiently. You will also need good plans to follow. Ideally, you should get your plans from a proven resource.

One good resource is Ted's Woodworking Plans which contains over 15,000 woodworking plans. It also has a ton of woodworking tips and information to help you become a better woodworker. There's something for everyone here. This is an online bestseller that has sold thousands and thousands of copies and it has helped more woodworking enthusiasts than any other product out there.

**Tip #1 – Get the Basics Right**
**Tools**
There's a saying that goes, "A poor workman always quarrels with his tools." While that is true, the fact remains that even a poor workman needs tools. If you want to be a good woodworker, not only do you need the right skills… but you also need the right tools.

The type of tools you pick will often depend on your skill level and temperament. Some people enjoy the process of manually working with their hands and taking time to create their masterpieces. Others want speed and efficiency so that they can get the job done quickly.

If you're the type who likes speed, you may need to invest in power tools to speed up the process. If you're the type who likes to do things slow, you can just stick to hand tools and whittle away at the wood. There is no right or wrong answer here.

Generally, though, it would be a good idea for beginners to stick to hand tools so that they build their skills. Some woodworking skills are best executed with hand tools. So, it will be useful to not be totally dependent on power tools.

## Use good plans

You can easily find a ton of woodworking plans online. However, many of them will not be good. The dimensions may be off or the instructions may be wrong. After all the effort, the finished product may not look like what you wanted it to look like. Usually, people blame themselves for this when in reality; the fault could lie with the inaccurate plans. You would be wise to choose one of Ted's tested and proven Woodworking Plans and follow through with that.

## Plan before proceeding

Once you decide on a plan, make sure you stay organized. Plan it well so that you have all the tools you will need for the project and also all the raw material to create the product. You must be well-prepared.

It's best to get it all sorted out first instead of starting on a project and halfway realizing that you are lacking certain tools or there is a shortage of wood, etc.

## Have a designated spot

Make sure you have one particular spot where you do your woodworking. It should be spacious enough for you to move around freely without obstruction. There should be good lighting, a safe area and your tools should be within easy reach.

Most people choose to either work in their garage or backyard. It's not a good idea to do woodworking within your house because of the dust and wood shavings which will get all over the place and will probably make your spouse furious.

## Keep an eye on your budget

Any experienced wood worker will know that woodworking will save you money but it isn't necessarily cheap. While creating your own furniture may be cheaper than buying it, there are still expenses involved. You will need to purchase the raw material and maybe even a few tools.

So, plan it all out so that you start on a project that is within your means. You don't want to end up in a situation where the project ends up halfway done because you don't have the budget to buy more raw materials. Knowing your budget will also allow you to shop around to get the best deal instead of just buying stuff blindly.

## Take accurate measurements

Woodworking requires a certain degree of precision. This is especially true if you're creating finger or dovetail joints. Make sure you take correct measurements and follow the plans to the letter. Attention to detail is crucial. One good practice will be to mark the wood so that you know where to cut or join, etc.

Introduction

**Adopt safety measures**

This is a very, VERY important point. Many people have injured themselves during woodworking because they were careless or they did not practice good safety. Anytime you're using power tools, you must be very alert and cautious.

You will need eye and ear protection. You may need to remove rings, chains or other jewelry that may get in the way. Make sure the blade on your power tool is well-secured and always disconnect the power when not in use. This topic of safety is so important that it will be covered in greater detail further down.

**Tip #2 – Know What Tools You Need for Wood Carving**

Wood carving is a technique where you create beautiful objects by whittling away at the wood. Unlike normal carpentry which involves sawing and hammering, wood carving is usually less strenuous and usually requires you to use a carving tool to shape the product.

**Tip #3 – Learn How to Bend Wood**

Knowing how to bend wood is a very useful skill to have. It's also something that most laymen have no idea about. They often wonder how wood is bent to make canoes, bows, etc. The truth of the matter is that bending wood is an easy process if you know how to do it.

There are 3 most commonly used methods of bending wood, we'll take a look at each one now.

Laminated Bending Wood

This is a very common method that is frequently used in furniture making. The way this method works is by gluing thin strips of wood, bending them and gluing them together. The thinner the wood, the easier it is to bend it. After the gluing, it is placed in a mold so that the wood holds its curved form. Once the glue dries, the wood will be curved.

Steam Bending Wood

Steam is used to bend wood with this method. It is probably the most commonly used method of bending wood and has been in practice since ancient times.

To use this method, you'll need a steam box. The wood will be placed in a mold and there will be a hose that connects that connects it to another box containing water.

Microwave Bending Wood

This method is used by many woodworking beginners. It's simple, it can be done at home and it's effective.

You will need to wrap a wet towel around the wood that you wish to bend. Then place it in the microwave and heat it up for about 20 seconds. Depending on the heat and the moisture, you will be able to bend the wood quite easily after that. The only disadvantage here is that you can only use this for small projects because you are limited by the size of your microwave.

### Tip #4 – Build a Wood Lathe for Yourself

A wood lathe is very useful for most woodworkers and you can easily build one yourself. This report is not going to go in-depth as to how you can create one because of the technical detail.

You can learn how to create one from Ted's Woodworking Plans or you can do your research online and learn how to do it.

### Tip #5 to #7 – Woodworking Safety Tips to Remember

Safety is the MOST important thing when doing woodworking. Injuries are common and even a lapse in concentration or judgment can result in severe injury. People have been known to lose fingers just from a second of carelessness while handling a power tool.

That is why 3 tips in this report have been dedicated just to safety precautions. While these may seem like common sense, you'd be amazed to find out how many people neglect to take safety precautions. Common sense is a flower that doesn't grow in everybody's garden.

### Tip #5 – Wear safety equipment

Just like how it is mandatory to wear a hard hat when you go on a construction site, it is of paramount importance that you wear the necessary safety equipment when doing woodworking.

If you need to wear safety goggles, do ensure that you wear them. Assuming that you know what you're doing and that it's not necessary is just tempting disaster to occur. All it takes is a splinter to fly off at high speed right into one's eye for it to blind them permanently. This is a very real possibility if you're using power tools.

Use latex gloves if you handle glue or you're doing some varnishing. All these safety measures will safeguard you from possible accidents that are waiting to happen.

### Tip #6 – Power tools are not toys

These are very dangerous pieces of equipment in the wrong hands. You could be an expert woodworker who has years of experience but even then, you need to be alert at all times when handling power tools. Never be over-confident!

Make sure to disconnect the cord from the power outlet when the power tools are not in use. Disconnecting it is better than merely turning off the power. Always do this when you're changing the blades of your power tools. Make sure your blades are sharp so that they slice through the wood like a hot knife through butter. If your blades are dull like a bowling ball, they are going to jerk and kick back when you use the power tools. This is very dangerous.

**Tip #7 – Work mindfully**

Do not engage in woodworking if you're drowsy or sleepy. Avoid using power tools if you're on medication that may leave you feeling sluggish or less than alert. Work in a place free from distractions.

If you have children, make sure to isolate yourself and lock the door while woodworking. You do not want your child running into your working area while you're handling power tools. This is disaster waiting to happen and there are real-life events that have occurred that are downright heartbreaking and it's all because safety precautions were not taken.

If you follow the 7 tips in this short report, you will be off to a good start when it comes to woodworking. However, this report is just scratching the surface of woodworking.

Woodworking Projects

## SIMPLE PLANS FOR BEGINNERS

### 1. Living Room Box

The living room box is just something that you can make to store remote controls in or anything else. It has a removable lid without hinges.

**Materials and Tools:**
- Hand Drill
- Hand Sander
- Speed Square
- Saw
- Clamps
- Strap Clamp
- Tape Measure
- Table Saw
- Drill Press
- Chisel Set
- Screw Driver
- Miter Box and Saw
- Wood (4' 1x4)
- Scrap Wood
- ¼ Inch Wood Dowel
- Screws
- Wood Glue
- Ruler

**Steps:**
1) From the end, measure:
   - (4) 4 7" long Boards
   - (2) 5" Boards
   - 8 ½" Board
2) Remember, a saw cuts wood by removing a small channel of the material, so measure after each cut rather than all at once.
3) Clamp the piece of wood into the miter box and measure from the one inch mark of your tape measure for it to be more accurate.
4) Do not sand any rough edges before you glue. You'll wreck the straight edge and there will be gaps when you're finished.
5) Take one of your seven-inch pieces and put a thin layer of wood glue on the long edges.
6) Place two more of the seven-inch boards on the glued edges and make a 'U' shape.

Simple Plans for Beginners

7) Clamp the ends loosely to hold everything together.
8) Put the final seven-inch board at the top without glue and put a clamp there to hold it in place. This is to make sure the edges are in line on both sides.
9) Tighten your clamps and be sure nothing has slid around. Now, let it dry for an hour.
10) When it's dry, remove your clamps and set the un-glued seven-inch board aside.
11) Place a layer of glue on the 'U' shaped edges and put both end caps on.
12) Place the clamp on both ends caps and let it dry overnight.
13) Remove the clamps.
14) Use your seven in board you didn't glue and check to see if it fits inside the top. It should be close, but not too tight.
15) Take your final 8 ½ inch board and measure out a line on either side that is ¾ of an inch in. The seven-inch piece should have exact measurement to fit.
16) Glue one side of the seven inch board and put it between the lines on the 8 ½ inch board. Clamp it down so it doesn't slip around.
17) When the glue has dried, unclamp it and see if the lid fits.
18) Sand and paint.

## 2. Hinged Box
**Materials and Tools:**
- Measuring Tape or Ruler
- Miter Box and Saw or Table Saw
- Wood Glue
- Clamps
- Wood – (1) four-foot 1x4
- One Nail, 2" Long
- Drill with Two bits
- Sand Paper
- Scrap Lumber

Cut the board into the following sizes:
- (3) 6" Pieces
- (2) 4 ¼" Pieces
- (1) 7 ½" Piece
- (2) ¾" by ¾" Blocks
- (1) 3" by ¾" Block, Round one end with a sander or sandpaper.

**Steps:**
1. Box

a. Begin with your two six inch pieces and glue them together in an 'L" shape. The edges should be lined up carefully.
   b. Clamp that and let it dry for an hour.
   c. Unclamp and glue the two end pieces.
   d. Clamp the ends in place and let dry for an hour.
   e. Unclamp and glue on the last six inch piece.
   f. Clamp and let dry overnight.
2. Hinge and Top
   a. Take the ¾" square block, just one, and the 3" by ¾" block with the rounded end, and drill through the center with a larger drill bit.
   b. Take the final ¾" block and drill through the center with the smaller bit.
   c. Test fit the screw by passing it through the larger holed block and into the smaller holed block. Do not tighten anything.
   d. Leave the pieces assembled.
   e. Place your 7 ½" piece on top of the finished box so that you have a level surface for the hinge assembly.
   f. Find the mid-point of the back, vertical piece and mark it with a sharpie. It should be at three inches.
   g. Glue the two squares in place and tighten. When it's settled, remove the screw, three inch block, and the top piece.
   h. After the glue has set, reassemble the three inch block and top, and leave the clamps in place.
   i. Make sure the top is square and glue the three inch block down. Be sure that the glue is away from the back edge.
   j. Let it dry overnight.
   k. Unclamp in the morning and see if everything is working smoothly.
   l. Remove the top before sanding and paint as desired.

Simple Plans for Beginners

## 3. Wooden Chopping Board

**Materials Required:**
- Tasmanian Oak (1 x 3.0m x 42mm x 19mm)
- Meranti (1 x 2.7m x 42mm x 19mm)
- Aquadhere External Adhesive (1 x 500ml)
- 1 Small Paint Brush
- A Bucket of Water and Old Newspaper Rag
- Small scraps of timber

**Tools Required:**
- 2 Clamps 250mm
- Carpenters square
- Cork sanding block
- Hand saw
- Sanding block - course, medium and fine sandpaper
- Hand plane

**Steps:**

STEP 1: Determine the width and length of your desired chopping board and this one measures 400mm (L) × 250mm (W).

STEP 2: Divide the width by 19 that is the width of the timber (250/19 = 13.15). To have the same color timber on either edge you will need an odd number of pieces (13 pieces).

STEP 3: Choose the color of timber you will want for the outside edges (7 light colored and 6 dark colored).

STEP 4: Cut your pieces to length and then place them on a flat surface (42mm side facing down) in an interchanging color pattern.

Woodworking Projects

STEP 5: You then apply aqua here exterior to all pieces except the last one and spread the glue with a brush to ensure complete coverage.

STEP 6: Stand all pieces on edge with a glue covered edge facing a row side of timber.

STEP 7: You then bring all pieces together even the one at the end that you didn't apply glue to.

STEP 8: With a carpenter's square get the ends straight but you can also use your eye.

STEP 9: Apply clamps using some excess pieces to stop the clamps from making moving or to make it stable. Make sure you are pressing down in order to get the pieces even before a final constriction.

STEP 10: With clamps in place and board leveled turn it over and remove paper bucking which may be stuck on the back of the board.

STEP 11: Lastly use a wet rag to wipe off extra glue that has clutched on both sides of the board. When you have removed all glue wipe off with a dry cloth to take away any extra water.

4. **Mirror Frame**

**Materials and Tools:**
- Birch Plywood
- Chair Rail that has a notch cut into the back
- Molding
- Glue
- Wood Screw

- Circular Saw
- Nail Gun and Nails
- Mirror
- Paint Brush
- Paint
- Wire Chain

**Steps:**

STEP 1: Choose a wood that you would like to use for making your frame. You can use oak if you have a dark room or use pine that will help you to lighten the space. If you have light in your room then you can use redwood, cherry or even mahogany which are woods that are darker. Or use birch plywood to save on cost.

STEP 2: Get the mirror you are making the frame for and lay it down on the wood (birch plywood) then trace the dimensions it has on the plywood's center.

STEP 3: Remove the mirror then cut out the dimensions you marked.

STEP 4: Cut a chair rail that will help the notch to fit tightly within the plywood's opening. Glue and screw the chair rail to the boarder of the frame which is inside and make sure the notch of the chair rail is inside the edge and this will help to keep the mirror from falling through the front of the frame.

STEP 5: Take the large molding and cut it and make it go around the outside of the mirror frame then glue and nail it in place.

STEP 6: Paint the frame.

STEP 7: Attach a board to the back of the frame by the use of a screw gun to hold the mirror in place.

STEP 8: Lastly, at the back of each side of the mirror frame screw in a large metal chain that will assist you to hang the mirror. Ensure that the metal chain is thick for it to offer extra support.

5. **Wine Rack**

**Materials:**
- Clamps
- Drill or screwdriver
- Screws
- 1 piece of ¼ inches x 2 feet x 4 ft. sanded plywood panel
- 1 piece of 1 inch x 2 inches x 8 feet select pine board
- Paint brush
- Paint or varnish

## Steps:

STEP 1: The following are basic steps usually involved when you're building a simple wine rack out of wood.

STEP 2. Measure the desired bottle container, prepare the necessary measurements and cut it according to the desired plan.

STEP 4: If you are deciding to use a screw, it will be best to pre-drill the wood to hold the rack together and to avoid it form splitting.

STEP 5: After drilling the wood, make the frame. Form it in crisscross and make sure that the connections were secured enough if the screws were not enough it is advisable to put some wood glue in it.

STEP 6: For the wine bottle support, racks, partial circles, arches or round holes can cradle each bottle. If it supports the neck bottle use a drill press to cut two different size holes- smaller arch for the neck and larger arch for the bottom of the wine bottle. Measure the diameter of the neck and bottom of the bottle to make accurate arches.

STEP 7: Use sander for smooth finish and apply final paint or varnish, whichever you desire.

# SHELVES (BEGINNERS PLAN)

Shelves are relatively easy to do and they are extremely useful, too. So, to get started, here are some amazing DIY shelf projects that you can do:
This is an easy and useful woodworking project that you can complete in an hour or two.

1. **Floating Shelves**

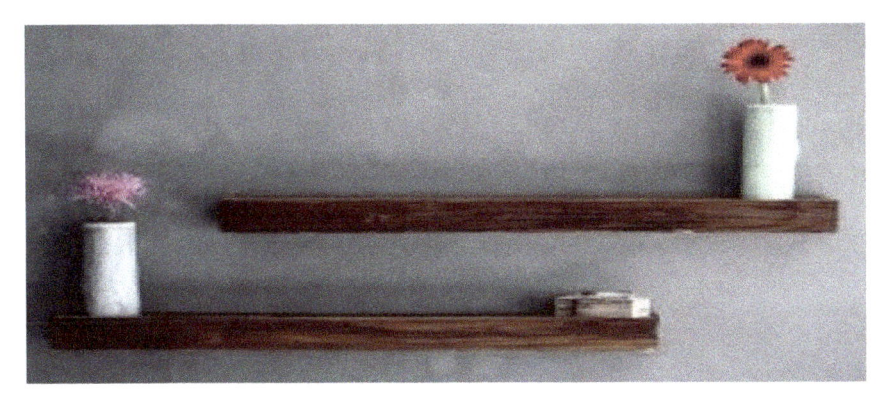

**MATERIALS:**
- Clamps
- Drill or screwdriver
- Screws
- 2 pieces of ¼ inches x 2 feet x 4 ft. sanded plywood panel
- 2 pieces of 1 inch x 2 inches x 8 feet select pine board
- Stud finder
- Level
- Paint brush
- Painter's tape with Edge
- Paint or varnish

**STEPS:**
STEP 1: Cut the wood pieces below into the following dimensions. To have the precise size you can just ask assistance from the staff of any depot store or hardware store you will visit for these materials.

- 4 – 1-in. x 2-in. x 21-in.
- 8 – 1-in. x 2-in. x 6½ in.
- 4 – ¼-in. x 8-in. x 21-in.
- 4 – ¼-in. x 2-in. x 8-in.
- 2 – ¼-in. x 2-in. x 21⅜-in.

Woodworking Projects

STEP 2: Screw these wood pieces together to make your frame. Your frame should look like this:

STEP 3: Glue, nail, or clamp the sanded panels to the frame. Attach the shelf to the using a screw driver. Then, screw at least one stud finder for stability.

STEP 4: Once you're certain that the shelf is leveled, add the remaining screws. Then, attach the second floating shelf. Make sure that it has the same measurements.

STEP 5: Attach the 1 inch by 2-inch boards to the front of both shelves. Glue the remaining ¼ inch boards to the front. Once the glue is dry, paint the shelves.

This project is fun and it is really easy to do. You can place these shelves in your bathroom, bedroom, or living room.

2. **Honeycomb Shelves**

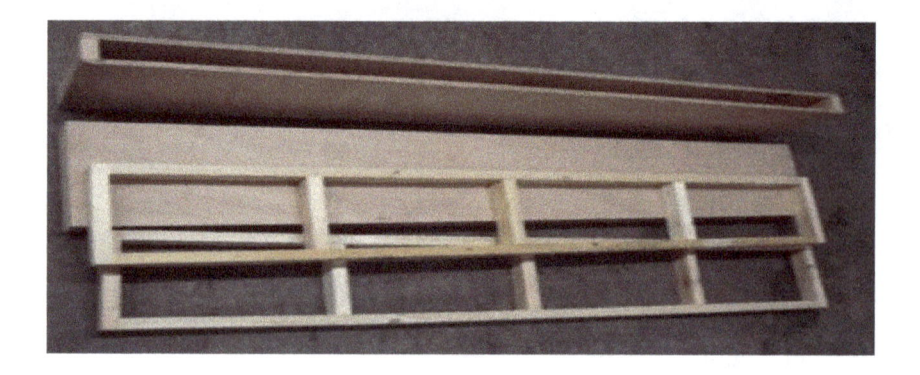

Honeycomb shelves are easy on the eyes and you can place just about anything on them – books, figurines, scented candles, and porcelain decors.

**Materials and Tools:**
- Miter saw
- Wood screws
- Drill
- Drill bit
- Level
- Rotary sander
- Tape measure
- Wall brackets
- Wood glue

Shelves (Beginners Plan)

- 3 Fencing planks
- Marker

**Steps:**

STEP 1: Set your miter saw to cut your planks at 30-degree angle. After you make the first cut, turn the plank over and measure the long ledge. Make sure that the long ledge is 12 inches. Mark the spot where you want to make your next cut. Then, make the second cut. You now have the first piece for your honeycomb shelves.

STEP 2: Repeat the process. You'll need to cut fifteen 12-inch pieces. Make sure that all 15 pieces have the exact same size.

STEP 3: To make one hexagon pod, you have to take 6 pieces of wood and set them standing on the floor. Connect these pieces to form a hexagon. You'll feel like you're connecting a puzzle. Use a wood club to connect the pieces together. Press the sides tightly.

STEP 4: Using a drill bit and a drill, pre-drill the holes when you want to screw and connect two hexagons together. This will make it easier for you to screw and it prevents the wood from cracking, too.

STEP 5: Repeat steps 3 and 4 until you're done with your first hexagon. Then, repeat the process until you've made three connected hexagons. Your honeycomb shelf should look like this:

STEP 6: To hang your shelf, find the studs and then screw your brackets into them. Screw the bottom part of the bracket first and then put some pressure to the top bracket. Make sure that it is durable and it can hold some weight.

STEP 7: Rest your shelf on the bracket. Then, go ahead and mark where you'll put your next bracket. Put as many brackets as necessary for reinforcement. Now, you're done!

This honeycomb shelf is fun, attractive, and surprisingly easy to make. This is a project that you can do with your friends and even your kids.

### 3. Leather Strap Shelf

This is an awesome and chic shelf that will add a lot of personality to any room.

**Materials:**
- Screw gun
- Staple gun
- 1-inch wide leather strap
- 1x6 inch plywood
- Paint (Any color will do)

**Steps:**

STEP 1: Paint the plywood and let it dry for a few minutes.

STEP 2: Bring the ends of the 1-inch leather strap together. Fold the ends over twice. Then, fold the ends of the strap to the wall using a screw gun.

STEP 3: Slip the painted plywood into the leather loop. The leather strap should be at least three inches from the shelf end. Ask someone to hold the second leather strap and then slide the other end of the painted plywood into the second ribbon loop.

STEP 4: Use a level to ensure that the shelf is straight. Then affix the second leather strap into the wall using a screw gun. Secure the leather straps under the plywood using a staple gun.

Shelves (Beginners Plan)

Remember that this shelf can only hold light objects so try not to put heavy and breakable objects on it.

## 4. Woodwork Plan for a Basic Bookshelf

This woodwork plan is perfect for beginners. You do not need a lot of tools to get this done. This project is incredibly easy to do, this could even be your first wood work project.

**Materials:**
- Router
- Electric drill
- Power sander
- Cut off saw
- 2 pieces of 1 x 12 and ¾ of an inch-thick pine wood
- 4 pieces of 1 x 11 and ¾ of an inch think pine wood
- 1 piece of 1 x 4 wood
- Table saw
- Clamps

Woodworking Projects

- Carpenter's square
- Deck screw
- 4d finish nails
- Tape measure
- Wood glue
- Screw gun
- Screws
- ¾" nail for the back

**Steps:**

STEP 1: Sand the wood pieces to improve the texture.

STEP 2: The longer pieces (1 x 12) will be the upright. So you need to cut a little dado or a slot. It has to be ¾ wide and ¼ inch deep. This will give a place for the shorter shelf boards to go up into the wood and be securely connected to the longer wood.

STEP 3: Cut the two dadoes across the boards using a router. You can also do this with a table saw if you don't have a router.

STEP 4: Sand again the dadoes using a power sander. After the wood is sanded, assemble the shelves using a wood glue. Place the glue on the bottom of the dadoes to give an added strength. Then place the boards into the dado slots. Start on one edge and then wiggle it around. Use a hammer to secure the shelf into the dado slots. Clamp it in tight to let the glue set. Clamp it overnight.

STEP 5: Take out the clamp. You may need to put a little reinforcement so put in screws in on the side using a screw gun.

STEP 6: Put the back onto the shelf. Cut it according to the length and width of your shelf and then nail it to your shelf. If you want, you can paint your shelf.

# BENCHES, CHAIRS AND STOOLS
# (INTERMEDIATE PLAN)

## 1. Work Bench

If you're serious about woodworking, then you should have a sturdy work bench. Here's a work bench that you can build in less than a day.

**Materials:**
- 2x2s for the frame and legs
- 2 x4 lumber for the frame
- 1/4" plywood that would serve as a workbench top
- Circular saw
- Bar clamps
- Chisel
- Square
- Hand drill
- Screws
- Wood glue

**Steps:**

STEP 1: Cut the legs. The length has to be 78 centimeters long. Use a measuring tape and a pencil to mark the wood.

STEP 2: Now, you need to cut the pieces that connect the legs. Cut four 2 x 4 pieces that's about 55 centimeters long. Then, assemble the frame by screwing and nailing the pieces together.

STEP 3: Then, drill on each edge of the frame and attach the legs. Then, place the screws in the pre-drilled holes.

STEP 4: Then, screw the rails to the legs. It's easier to do this if the bench is lying on its side.

STEP 5: Cut the plywood to fit the size of the frame. Then, screw the top of the workbench from the below.

Now you're done! This workbench only cost around $15! Think of all the money that you'll be saving when you make your own furniture.

2. **Three-Legged Stool**

**Materials:**
- Pine log
- Screws
- Power Sander or Sand Paper
- Varnish
- Band saw
- Planer
- Three aspen logs

- Knife
- 3 aspen logs
- Hammer
- Nails

**Steps:**
STEP 1: Cut a piece of wood from the log using a chainsaw
STEP 2: Trim the wood into about two inches thick.
STEP 3: Mark a circle on the wood and cut the circle using a band saw
STEP 4: Then, flatten the surface using a planer. Then cut three 14 inch aspen logs. This will serve as the legs of your stool.
STEP 5: Peel the aspen logs using a knife. Then, sand them.
STEP 6: Nail the legs to pine log using a hammer. Then, paint the stool with varnish. Let it dry.

Now, you have a stool! You can make as many stools as you like.

3. **Simple Chair**

This is a simple 2 x 4 chair plan that you can implement in just a few hours.
Dimensions
17 ½" x 18 1/2" x 37 ¼"

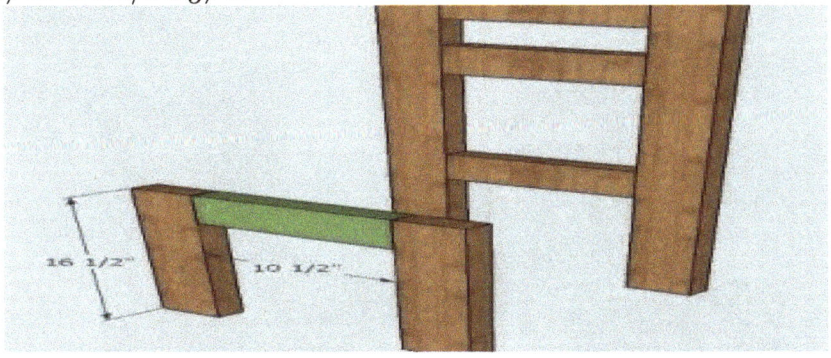

Woodworking Projects
**Materials:**
- 2 pieces of 10 feet long 2x4s
- 1 piece of 8 feet long 2x4
- Drill
- Saw
- 2 ½" screws
- 4" screws
- Wood filler
- Wood glue
- Paint
- Sander

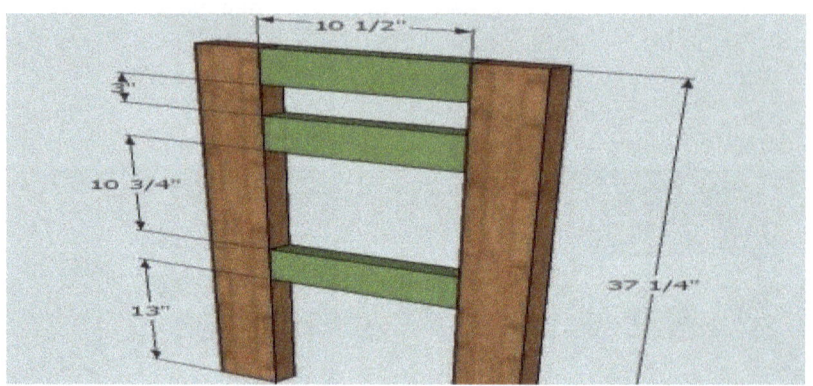

Cut List
- A – 2 pieces of 37 ¾ for back legs
- B – 4 pieces of 10 ½" for back and front boards
- C – 2 pieces of 16 1/2" for the front legs
- D - 2 pieces of 15" side boards
- E - 1 piece 13 ½"
- F – 3 pieces of 18 ½" for the seat
- G – 2 pieces of 17" for the seat side

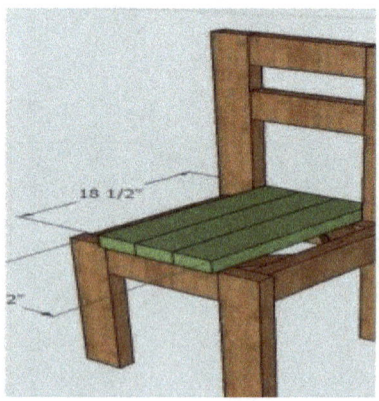

**Steps:**
STEP 1: Build the back.
The first step is to build the back of the chair. You would need to grab the 2 back legs and three front and back boards. Then assemble them following the illustration below. Connect the front and back boards to the legs using 2 ½ pocket screws and Kreg jig. You can also use wood glue.
STEP 2: Assemble the front.
After you build the back, you need to assemble the front using the front legs and the back piece as shown in the picture below:
STEP 3: Assemble the chair.
Use the side board pieces to connect the front and back sections. Screw these pieces into the front and back parts of the chair using a screw gun. Use the illustration below as a guide:
STEP 4: Add the support.
Install a 13 1/2 "long at the back of the seat opening. This will give the seat boards an extra space to sit on.

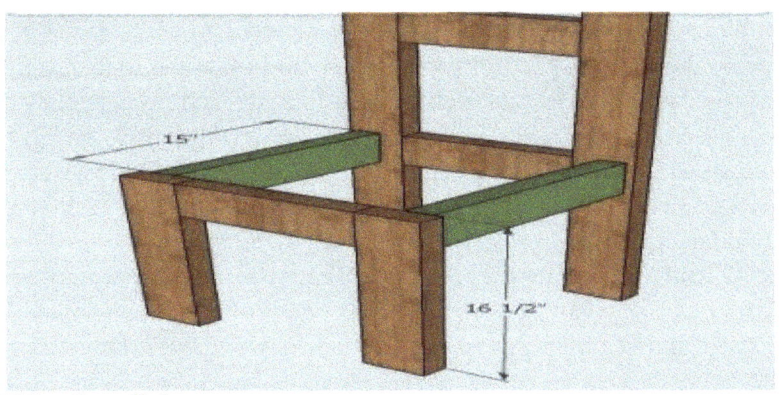

STEP 5: Install the seat.
Attach the seat boards using wood glue and screws. Follow the illustrations below.
STEP 6: Finish up.
Sand the chair and then apply some paint.

# WOODWORKING PROJECTS FOR KITCHEN (ADVANCE PLAN)

1. **Under sink storage:**

To increase the storage space for your kitchen, the best way is to make under sink storage system. Many cabinets are not fully utilized because they are inaccessible. The under-sink cabinet is usually ignored because you have to kneel down with the help of a torch to search for stuff over there. Here we are providing you way to construct an easy to pull out drawers that can accommodate a lot of item with the ease of easy accessibility.

First of all, you need to measure the areas where you want to accommodate these drawers. These can be a single drawer or multiple drawers depending on the space and need. These can also be made to pull them around sides of pipes.

**Materials:**
- 2-ft. X 2-ft. Of 1/2-inch Plywood
- Half sheet of 3/4-inch hardwood plywood
- Two linear ft. of 1-inch x 6-inch maple,
- Linear ft. of 1-in. X 4-inches Maple
- 1-5/8-inches screws
- Four pairs of 20-inches ball-bearing slides
- Wood glue
- Drill
- Measuring tape
- Saw
- Things for writing
- Sand paper

**Steps for The Space Drawers:**
- Measure the space where you want to make the drawers.
- Make a base from the wood which will be a ¼ inch wide (for A).
- Make the drawer 1 inch narrower than the indentation between the partitions
- Cut all the drawer parts.
- Sand them with sand paper and apply two coats of finish material.
- Set the drawer slides on 3/4-inches spacer levelled with the front border of the indentation (B).
- Attach them to the indentation and fix them with screws.
- Set the other drawers in the same manner on ¾ inches spacer to create an appropriate and connect them with the help of the screws to the side of the tray levelled to the front.
- Now attach the base to the bottom of the cabinet and fix it with the help of the screws
- Now glide these drawers inside the cabinet

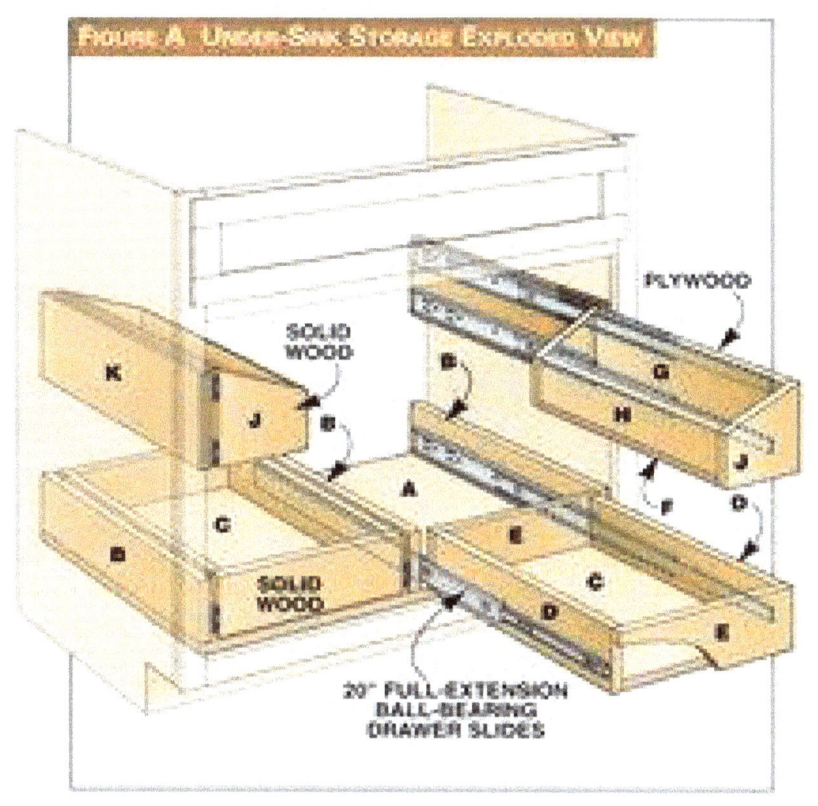

**Steps for The Side Drawers:**
- For making of the side drawer, you have to flow these steps

Woodworking Projects

- First of all, you need to make cleats (K) for they support of side drawers, and they should be in level with each other. Keep the measurement accurate, so when you will be pulling them out, so they do not get stuck because of hinges of the door of the cabinets.
- Attach all the parts of the drawer with the help of screws and wood glue.
- The slides need to be attached to the sides with the help of screws and glue. Make sure they are strongly attached.
- After finishing all this work scrap the sides of the wood with the help of sand paper.

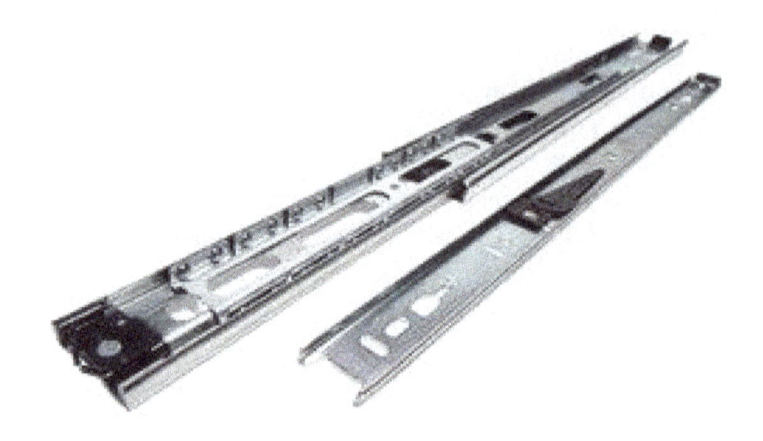

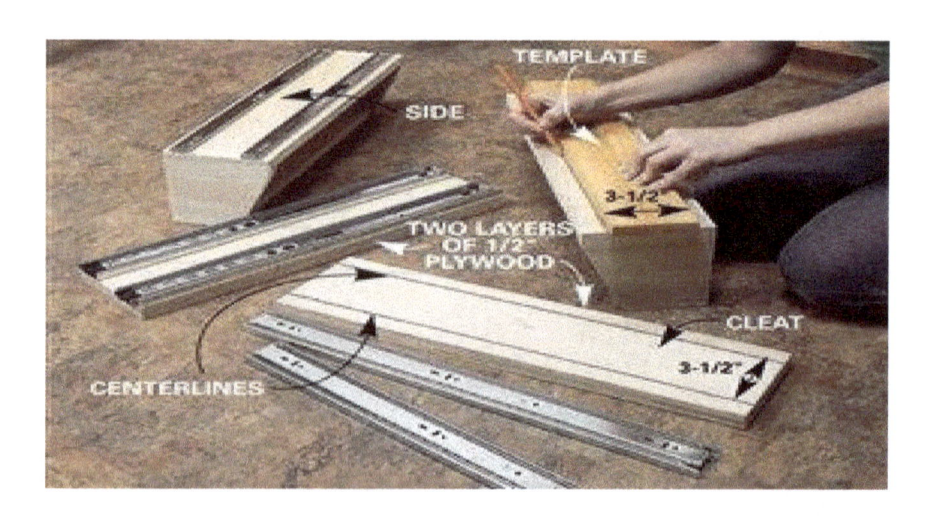

~30~

**Final Assembly:**
- First of all, you need to build a base for the support of the bottom drawers.
- This base is assembled in the bottom of the cabinet just behind the hinges of the door of the cabinet.
- This will need you to cut a piece of wood of the size of the bottom of the cabinet and fix it with the help of screw behind the hinges.
- The front edge of the base should be in alignment to the frame.
- Now attach the slides on the side of the side drawers.
- Make a 3 ½ inches template on the cleat and the long side of each wood piece.
- Make outline of this template
- Make holes around these marking lines with the help of drill
- Now attach the cleats on the side walls of the cabinet with the help of screws. For temporary holding of this cleat, you can use a plywood spacer.
- Assemble all the drawers at their places. Your under-sink storage is ready.

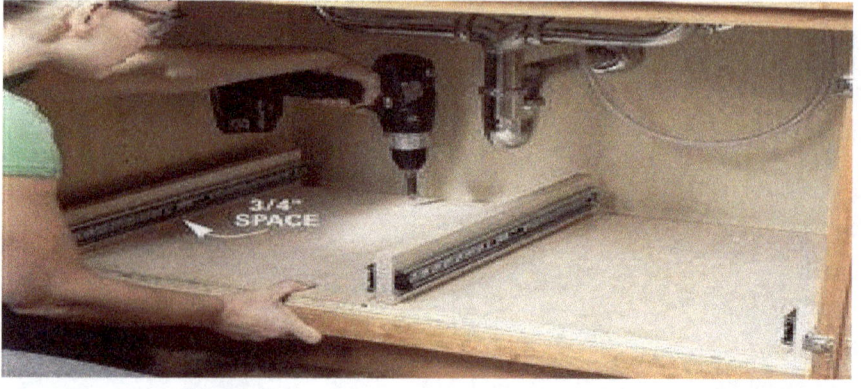

## 2. Hanging Pot Rack

Hanging pot rack is the need of every kitchen and present in every house. The biggest advantage they provide is that they allow accommodating a large number of pots in a compact space.

Hanging pot rack can be easily made at home with the help of easily available material and very easy techniques with less time consumption.

**Materials:**
- Hardwood
- Bar clamps
- Saw
- Sandpaper
- Steel wool
- Measuring tape
- Square
- Paintbrushes
- Metal file
- 1-1/2" brad nails
- Four screw hooks
- S-hooks
- 3/8-inch wooden furniture buttons
- Wood glue
- 135 x 15-foot chain
- 1-5/8" screws

- Two screw hooks
- 1x2 x 6' board
- Polyurethane
- 1x3 x 6' board
- Stain
- 1x2 x 4' board
- Copper pipe
- Wood filler
- 18 x 1 1/4-inch wire brads

**Steps:**
- First of all, you will need to cut all the wood in the desired lengths as provided above with wood of your choice.
- File the end of the copper wire after cutting
- Clean the pipe with the help of steel wool and make sure to rub in one direction and along the length of the pipe. This will give a lustre to the pipe.

Making of rails:

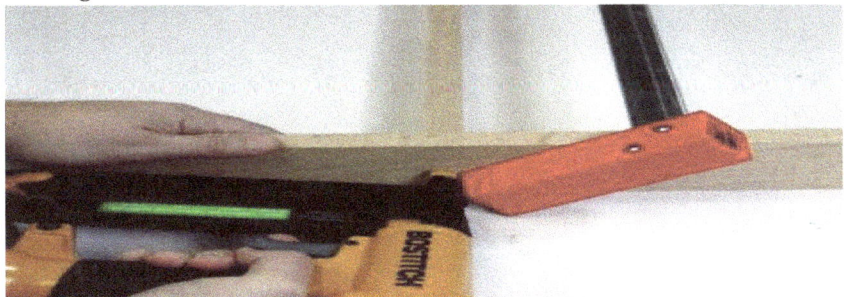

- With the use of the first image cut the side rails

Woodworking Projects

- With the help of the second image, make the drill hole in the rails to support them on the main.

- Start attaching the support rail at the level with the bottom edge in accordance with the angle that has been cut with its centre on one side of the rail.
- Attach the rails with the help of screws and wire brads
- Repeat this step for the second side of the assembly.
- Now start positioning the other support rails at the level with the bottom edge. Strengthen them with the help of glue and wire brads.

Assembling of the base:

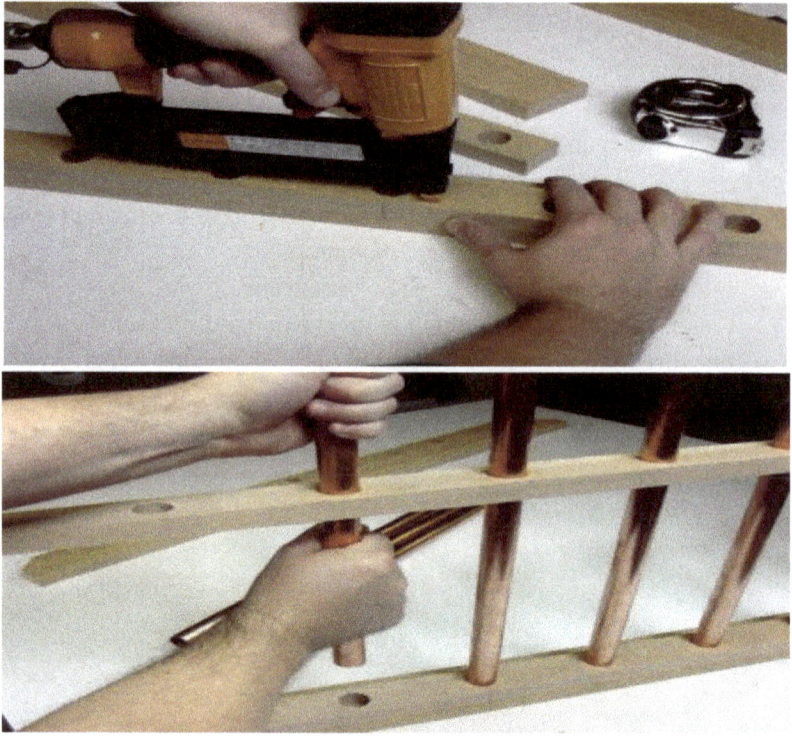

- Start positioning the end rails in the level with the bottom edge of one side rail and opposite to the ends of the support rail attached to

the side rail. These should be all levelled so that the support rail is at the bottom.
- Start making the hole of 3/8 inch and attach 3/8 in the furniture button onto it and strengthen them with the help of screws and glue.
- Cut the copper wire in the listed dimension above.
- Now insert the copper wire into the holes made in the support rails. For passing those with ease apply wax or liquid soap on them.
- The remaining sides of the rail are assembled with its rail support level against the side rails and copper pipe.

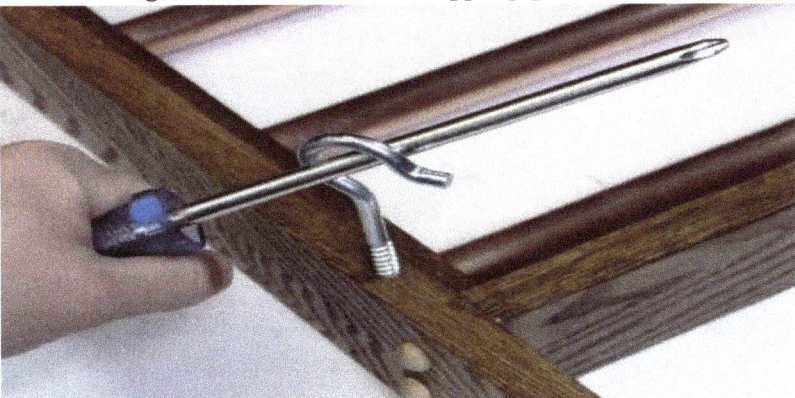

- Now make countersunk holes with the help of drill of 3/8 inch size. Fix them with the help of glue and screws.
- Now apply glue to furniture buttons where they are attached and insert them into the screw holes of side rails.
- Now fill any hole left due to nails, sand or stain
- Apply polyurethane
- Drill four holes for the screw eyes 3 1/2 inches from the ends of the side rails.
- Now drive the screw eyes till the whole threads are driven inside
- The hanging pot rack is ready

Hanging Up:
These can be hanged to the joist depending upon the placement of the screw eyes and length of the joist.

Woodworking Projects

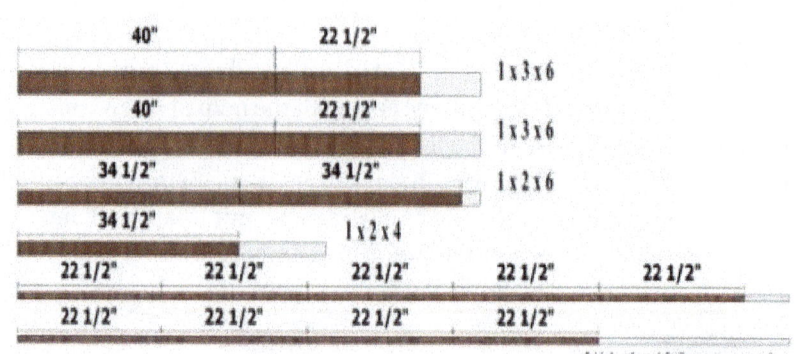

| | |
|---|---|
| 40"  22 1/2" | 1 x 3 x 6 |
| 40"  22 1/2" | 1 x 3 x 6 |
| 34 1/2"  34 1/2" | 1 x 2 x 6 |
| 34 1/2" | 1 x 2 x 4 |
| 22 1/2"  22 1/2"  22 1/2"  22 1/2"  22 1/2" | |
| 22 1/2"  22 1/2"  22 1/2"  22 1/2" | |

3/4-inch x 10-foot copper pipe

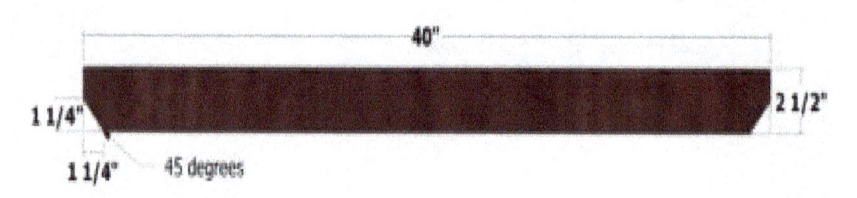

40"  2 1/2"
1 1/4"
1 1/4"  45 degrees

side rail

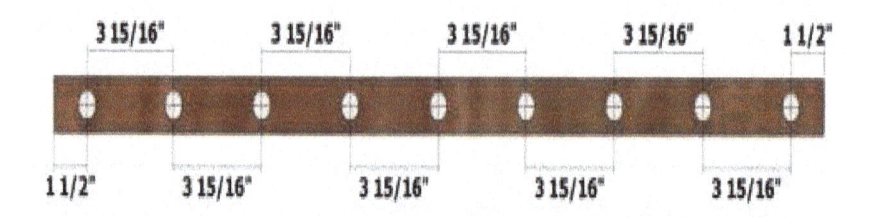

3 15/16"  3 15/16"  3 15/16"  3 15/16"  1 1/2"
1 1/2"  3 15/16"  3 15/16"  3 15/16"  3 15/16"

support rail

~36~

# BEDS (ADVANCE PLAN)

## 1. Queen Slat Bed
**Material List:**
- 2.5" and 1.25" Screws
- Glue
- 8- 6" hex bolts
- 1" Brad Nails
- 1 package of Bed Rail Hardware
- 3/4" Dowel or 14- 3/4" x 1" plugs or 14- 3/4" wood button plugs
- 2- 4x4x8
- 14- 1x4x8
- 2- 2x8x8
- 2- 2x6x8
- 10- 2x4x8
- 2- 2x2x8

**Tools Needed:**
- Miter Saw
- 1/4" drill bit (to drill at least a 5" deep hole)
- 3/4" Forstner drill bit
- 400 grit sanding block
- Finish Nailer (and Air Compressor)
- Oscillating Multi Tool or Japanese Flush Cut Saw
- Drill
- Table saw or Circular saw
- Rubber Mallet
- Square and Pencil and Measuring Tape
- Orbital Sander and a couple grits of sand paper (80, 120, 240)

Woodworking Projects

## Cut List:
- 2- 4x4x54" (headboard posts)
- 8- 1x4x58" (trim)
- 2- 4x4x21" (footboard posts)
- 2- 1x4x30" ripped to 2.75" (headboard slats)
- 2- 1x4x15" ripped to 2.75" (footboard slats)
- 15- 1x4x15" (footboard slats)
- 15- 1x4x30" (headboard slats)
- 2- 2x8x80" (side rails)
- 2- 2x4x65" (middle plate)
- 8- 2x4x60" (side rail slats)
- 2- 2x2x76" (side rail slat supports)
- 2- 2x6x67" (top plate)

## Steps:
STEP 1. Sand all the pieces of the project to smooth the boards, get rid of any imperfections, burrs, markings, and to slightly round off edges.

STEP 2. If you already know what color of stain you want to use, you can also stain each piece individually as well.

STEP 3. Lay the headboard slats (both D and E) down and in a row. Place the 2 ripped slats in random places to not draw attention to them. Have the best sides facing up.

STEP 4. Lay 2 of the trim boards (C) flush with the ends of the headboard slat boards. Glue the ugly side of the trim boards and nail them to the slats, be sure keep the slats tight and flush with the trim board.

STEP 5. Once the 2 trim boards are secure, flip the panel over and repeat. This time use 1.25" screws to secure the trim boards to the slats instead of finish nails.

STEP 6. Repeat the process for the footboard panel. Lay the footboard slats (both F and G) down and in a row. Place the 2 ripped slats in random places to not draw attention to them. Have the best sides facing up.

STEP 7. Lay 2 of the trim boards (C) flush with the ends of the footboard slat boards. Glue the ugly side of the trim boards and nail them to the slats, be sure keep the slats tight and flush with the trim board.

STEP 8. Once the 2 trim boards are secure, flip the panel over and repeat. This time use 1.25" screws to secure the trim boards to the slats instead of finish nails.

STEP 9. Allow the glue to dry on the panels by laying them face up for at least 30-60 minutes.

STEP 10. Lay the headboard posts (A) next to each other with the best sides facing up and out. Make 2 marks on the outside of each post at; 1.75" from the top end x .875" from the bottom face and 25.75" from the bottom end

Beds (Advance Plan)

and .875" from the bottom face. Make a 3/4" deep x 3/4" diameter hole in these places.

STEP 11. Lay the footboard posts (B) next to each other with the best sides facing up and out. Make 2 marks on the outside of each post at; 1.75" from the top end x .875" from the bottom face and 7.75" from the bottom end and .875" from the bottom face. Make a 3/4" deep x 3/4" diameter hole in these places.

STEP 12. Lay the headboard panel on the work surface face up. Align the headboard posts, so the holes line up in the middle of the trim and slat boards. Pre-drill a hole with a 1/4" drill bit around 5" deep into both the post and the panel. Glue the joint and then screw in the hex bolts.

STEP 13. When both posts are aligned and attached to the panel, repeat with the footboard. Lay the footboard panel on the work surface face up. Align the footboard posts, so the holes line up in the middle of the trim and slat boards. Pre-drill a hole with a 1/4" drill bit around 5" deep into both the post and the panel. Glue the joint and then screw in the hex bolts.

STEP 14. Stand the headboard and footboard up. Keep an eye on the joints and immediately wipe any glue that is dripping out of the joints (eventually, you will get skilled at knowing precisely how much or little glue to add to secure a joint with glue dripping).

STEP 15. Grab the middle plate boards (J) and line them up on top of the headboard and footboard. The middle plate should be flush with the width of the headboard and footboard.

STEP 16. Glue and screw the middle plates down. Avoid screwing them down in the exact middle of the length of the board, and the exact middle of the posts (you will need these spots for the top plate in the next step).

STEP 17. Lay the top plate boards (K) with the best side facing up. Mark the exact middle of the length and width of each board, as well as 2.75" from the end x 2.75" from the back edge on each end. Drill a 3/4" diameter x 3/4" deep hole at all 6 marks.

STEP 18. Grab the top plate boards and line them up on top of the middle board. They should overhang an inch all around, or you can make them flush with the back of the headboard to allow the bed frame to go flush up against the wall and the back of the footboard to not interfere with the mattress. Centered is more stable though.

STEP 19. Screw the top plate boards down.

STEP 20. Grab your dowel or button plugs. Glue the bottom edge and tap into each hole on the top plates and posts with a rubber mallet. If you used a dowel, use you oscillating saw or flush cut saw to cut the dowels flush, then sand over the area so it is smooth and no glue is present.

STEP 21. Set the headboard and footboard aside for now. Lay the side rails (H) with the best-looking side down.

STEP 22. Draw a few lines on the board 1" from the bottom edge. Then place a mark 2" from each end.

STEP 23. Align the side rail slat supports with these marks, glue and screw down every 10-16" along the board.

STEP 24. Assemble the Bed Rail Hardware onto the posts and slats according to the manufacturer's instructions. Make sure there is at least 60" between the side rails and no more than 61". Set it to whatever height you want the bed at. Keep in mind, this bed frame doesn't require a box spring since it has slats. If you want to still use a box spring you can forgo the slats that span from side rail to side rail as long as the span between the side rails is between 60" and 60.25" otherwise there is too much wiggle room.

STEP 25. Assemble the bed to make sure everything fits perfect.

STEP 26. From here you can do any staining (if you haven't already or touch ups from dowels), paint, or go straight to the finish. Allow the coats of finish to dry for several hours before applying another coat. Before the last coat of finish, sand the wood with 400 grit sand paper.

STEP 27. Lay 2 of the trim boards (C) flush with the ends of the headboard slat boards. Glue the ugly side of the trim boards and nail them to the slats, be sure keep the slats tight and flush with the trim board.

# INNOVATIVE CREATIONS

1. **Mini Desk Masterpiece**

**Materials and Tools:**
- Pallets
- Hammer
- Nails
- Stain
- Saw
- Sandpaper
- Pencil
- Measuring tape

**Steps:**
STEP 1: Start by removing all the wood on 1 side of your pallet. Measure your desk where the stand is going to be, and mark on your pallet where you need to cut. Follow these lines with your saw, then use sandpaper to sand down the wood so it's smooth.
STEP 2: Apply a stain to the wood now, bringing out the natural look.
STEP 3: Sand down any other rough spots, and your stand is done!

2. **Rustic Pallet Wagon**

**Materials and Tools:**
- Pallets
- Hammer
- Nails

- Stain
- Saw
- Pencil
- Measuring tape
- Wheels
- Rope

**Steps:**
STEP 1: Start by sanding down your pallet. You don't want any rough patches or potential slivers from the wood. Apply a stain.
STEP 2: Once the stay has dried, flip the pallet over, and use your pencil to mark where you want the wheels to be placed. Screw them in place securely.
STEP 3: For the handle, I recommend you purchase 2 hooks from your local hardware store and screw them in place right at the front of the wagon. Loop the rope through these hooks and tie securely. That's it! Your wagon is ready for anything.

## 3. Quirky Office Desk
**Materials and Tools:**

- Pallets
- Extra poles for the legs
- Paint
- Hammer
- Nails
- Stain
- Saw
- Pencil
- Measuring tape

**Steps:**
STEP 1: Remove all the wood from one pallet and cut the lengths of board in half. Screw these in place on the second pallet, then sand it down so you don't have to worry about splinters.

STEP 2: Make sure there are no cracks or rough spots, then stain. Once the stain has dried, flip the piece over.

STEP 3: Paint all 4 poles the color of your choice, and place them at equal distances at the bottom of your table. Screw securely in place.

STEP 4: Make sure there's no rough spots, and your new table is ready for action!

Woodworking Projects

## 4. Practical Pallet Chair

**Materials and Tools:**

- Pallets
- Hammer
- Nails
- Stain
- Saw
- Pencil
- Measuring tape

**Steps:**

STEP 1: Start by completely disassembling the pallet. You may need 2, so go ahead and take apart 2.

STEP 2: You are going to need 16 boards that are 2 feet long, cut these. You will also need 4 boards that are 4 feet long, 2 boards that are 3 feet long (cut these with their legs at an angle to sit on the floor) and 1 support board.

STEP 3: Sand all of these smooth, and lay them out. Use the photo as a reference, and screw all 16 boards at an angle, these are the seat of chair, use the screw both sets of 4-foot-long boards at right angles, then use the photo once more to see where to place the feet of the chair.

STEP 4: Screw the entire piece together, and apply a stain. Let dry, and use a cushion over the top.

## 5. Super Slim End Table

**Materials and Tools:**

- Pallets
- Hammer
- Nails
- Stain
- Saw

**Steps:**

STEP 1: This end table is incredibly easy to make. Simply cut 1 pallet down the center of each of the support pieces. Sand down and apply a stain, then stack up as you see in the photo.

STEP 2: Apply another stain, and screw in place. Let dry, and you are done!

# SMALL FURNITURE (BEGINNERS PLAN)

## 1. Bathroom Shelf Unit

**Materials and Tools:**

2- 3/4 X 6 1/2 X 32 side Lumber

1- 3/4 x 9 1/2 x 18 Top Rail

1- 3/4 x 5 1/2 x 18 Top Shelf

2- 3/4 x 5 1/4 x 18 mid and Bottom Shelves

1- 3/4 x 7 x 18 Bottom Rail

1- 5/8 diam. X 18 Towel Bar

No. 8 × 1 1/2" wood screws

**Steps:**

STEP 1:

- Once you have the boards cut to length, mark the profiles for the side pieces. Using the drawing on the facing page as a guide, you could mark the shape directly onto one board and cut it out with your jigsaw (if you are feeling confident). A more precise and safer method is to draw the shape on cardboard first and cut it out to be sure it looks okay, then trace it onto the board.

- After you have cut out one side piece, use it as a guide to trace the curve on the other side piece (or use the cardboard pattern, flipped over). This will guarantee that the two side pieces will have the exact same curves.

- Next draw the wavy shapes for the 18"-long top and bottom rails. To achieve symmetry in your design, take a 9"-wide piece of paper or cardboard and draw a curvy line on it. Cut out the design and trace it onto one half of the 18"-long board. Then flip over the cardboard and trace the design onto the other half of the board. Repeat the process for the bottom border, using a different curve (as shown in the drawing).

- When you're riding your jigsaw around the curves, guide the blade smoothly so you don't create bumps and dings that you'll have to sand out later. Many jigsaws have a dial that allows you to adjust the stroke of the blade to be either gentle or aggressive, depending on the wood you're cutting (and the mood you're in).

Small Furniture (Beginners Plan)

STEP 2:

- Next, cut out the crescent moon on the side pieces. (If you wish, you can skip this decorative detail.) Draw the shape where you want it (making sure it won't be in the same spot as the top rail or the top shelf) and drill a generous hole in the middle of the moon. Insert your jigsaw blade into that hole, and proceed to cut out the moon. You should definitely use a scrolling blade for this purpose. A scrolling blade is more delicate than a regular jigsaw blade and can handle tight corners that would make a standard blade buck.

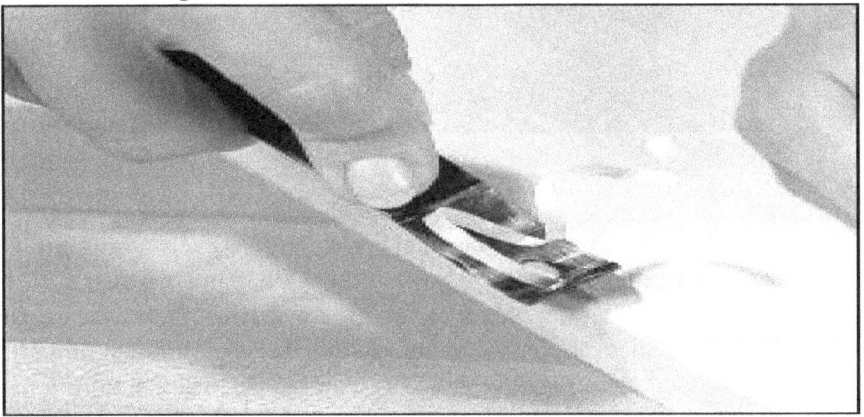

STEP 3:

- Once you've cut out all your pieces, round over the sharp edges with sandpaper. You could instead use a cornering tool to ease all the straight edges. A Veritas cornering tool makes short work of softening the edges of pine (see photo). If the blade chips or binds, you're working against the grain. Try pulling from the opposite end of the board. Grain lines always curve around knots, so you may have to change direction several times, but it's still faster than sanding.

STEP 4:

- It's tempting to screw the whole unit together right now, but there are several advantages to putting the stain, paint, or clear-coat on the individual pieces before you go any further. It is much easier than having to cover all the multiple surfaces of the shelf unit after it's assembled. Besides that, glue squeeze-out will glom on to bare wood during the assembly process, but if your boards already sport a coat of finish, the glue can easily be wiped off.

- The piece pictured here has been finished with shellac. Shellac has to be applied with a patient, steady hand in smooth, long strokes that don't overlap (see photo above). Because it's alcohol-based, it dries extremely fast, so there's little downtime. If you're mixing your own shellac, use a good solvent procured from a reliable woodworking supply store.

- Even if you don't work with shellac as your final finish, you can brush a couple of quick dabs of shellac on any knots. This will seal the knots and prevent sap from oozing up under your

Small Furniture (Beginners Plan)

chosen finish. In fact, shellac is a great primer coat for pretty much any finish except stain.

STEP 5:
- Now you're ready to "dry fit" the whole unit. Lay it all out with the sides, shelves, and borders in place. Clamp everything together lightly and square the shelves using a speed square. Make those clamps nice and tight. Use a pencil to mark a light line on the side pieces under each of the shelves for reference later when you're doing the final assembly under the duress of knowing that the glue is starting to set up.

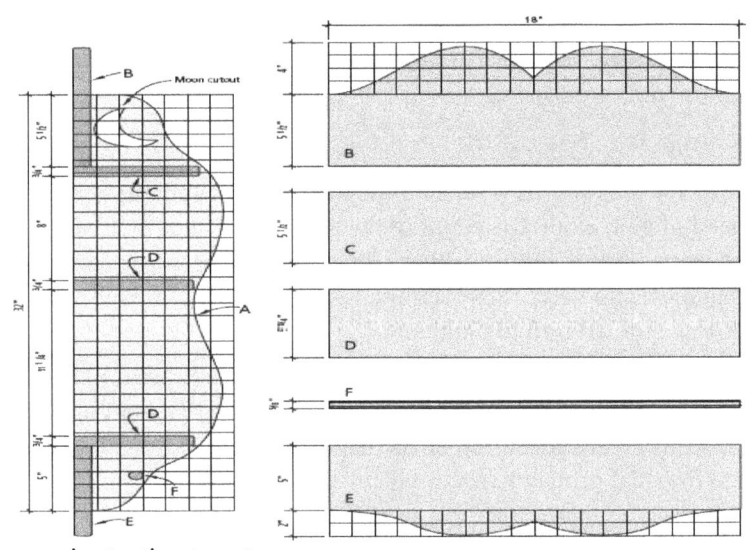

Woodworking Projects

STEP 6:

- While all the clamps are in place, predrill pilot holes for your screws so you don't split the shelves when you drive the screws. Then, right on top of the predrilled screw holes, drill larger holes to a depth of 3/8" to make a cavity for the plugs that will hide the screw heads. To avoid drilling the plug holes too deep, it's a good idea to wrap a piece of masking tape around your drill bit 3/8" from the end so you know when to stop (see photo).

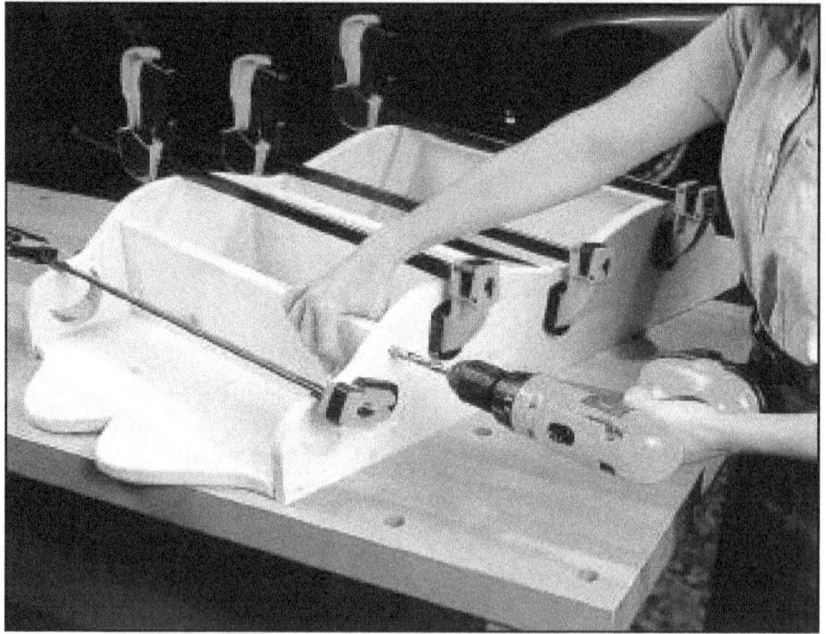

STEP 7:

- Now for the "wet fit." Take all the pieces apart and apply a modest bead of glue along the edges of the shelves and borders, plus a dab on each end of the towel bar. Reassemble and clamp everything together, and drive those screws. Use a damp rag to wipe away any oozing glue around the joints.

- To make plugs to cover the screw heads, you can use a plug-cutter bit. This is a device that fits into your drill just like a regular bit. It cuts tiny cylindrical wood plugs that camouflage the screw heads, so the finished project looks tidy.

- Once your screws are in place, fire up the plug-cutter and cut the plugs in a scrap piece of pine (see photo). Once you've cut about thirty plugs, use a knife or screwdriver to pop each plug out of its little hole.

Small Furniture (Beginners Plan)

- As an alternative to cutting your own plugs, you can buy precut hardwood plugs at the hardware store. This may be easier, but it has some downsides: the color of the wood won't match, and hardwood isn't as absorbent as pine so the plugs take finish differently and won't blend in.

STEP 8:

- Before inserting each plug into its predrilled hole, place a drop of glue on the bottom of each plug and smear it around a bit.
- When you have your unit plugged, wait twenty minutes for the glue to set up. Then use a flush-cut saw to cut each plug flush with the surface of the cabinet. If you don't have a flush-cut saw, you can take the plugs down fairly quickly using a sander loaded with 80-grit sandpaper. Once the plugs are cut and sanded, touch up the plugs and sides of your unit with shellac or whatever finish you're using.
- Now it's time to mount your unit on the wall. One mounting technique is to screw two 2"-long strips of metal plumber's tape (which has prepunched holes) on the back of the shelf unit, then lift the unit onto waiting nails anchored in studs above the toilet. Finding the studs is a matter of importance, because you don't want your unit to come crashing down on you at an unfortunate moment.

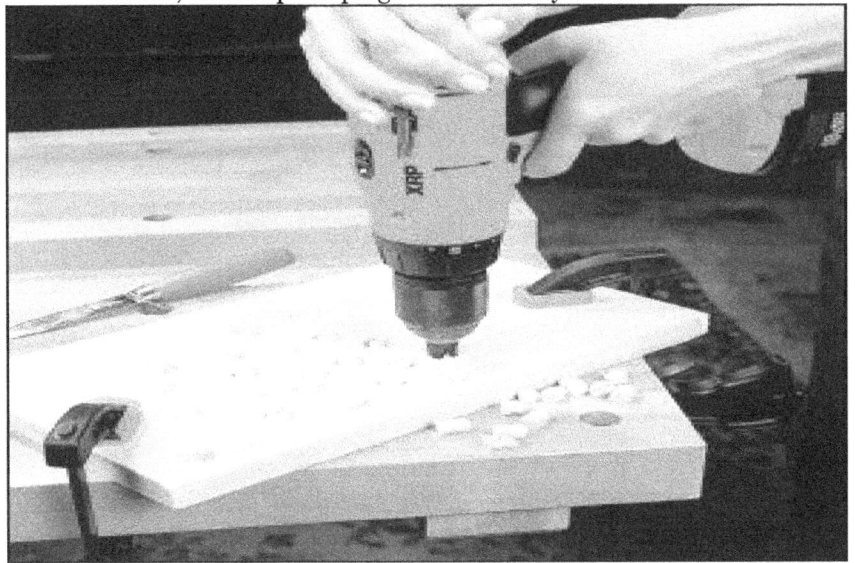

Woodworking Projects
## 2. Handy Box

This toolbox is perfect for holding all those everyday tools that you use around the house—a tack hammer, screwdrivers, tape ruler, extra screws and nails, etc.

The techniques used to make this box are simple and fun. The miter joints that are used here will require a table saw to cut all the 45° angles (a circular saw could be used, but would be much more difficult). Because of the large area of the beveled joint, a glue bond is sufficient to make a strong connection here. .

A clear finish was used in the pictured project in order to keep the wood visible. You can finish this project—and the others—as you like, with paint, stain, or whatever suits your needs.

Small Furniture (Beginners Plan)

**Materials and Tools:**
- 2- ¾ 6 X 16 Plywood Top and Bottom
- 2- ¾ x 7 ½ x 16 Plywood Front and Back
- 2- ¾ x 6 x 7 ½ Plywood End
- 1 continuous hinge (3/16" × 1½" × 16");
- 1 draw bolt;
- 1 screen door handle

**Steps:**
STEP 1:
- Cut all the parts to size as shown in the Materials List. Then tilt the table saw blade to 45° and attach a sacrificial fence to the saw's fence. Adjust this setup until you can cut a 45° bevel on the edge of the box parts. This setup allows you to cut bevels on parts that have already been cut to size, which is easier than trying to cut all the parts to size and bevel them at the same time.
- A safety note: Be careful when cutting and handling plywood after you've cut bevels on the edges. Plywood edges are fragile and can easily be chipped or nicked. Also, you could receive some nasty cuts from these edges because they are sharp.

STEP 2:
- Double-check the 45° bevel to be sure that a perfect 90° corner is formed. This is critical for all the parts to join together squarely at glue-up time.

STEP 3:
- Lay out the bottom A, the front and back B, and the two ends C face up as shown. Use clear packing tape to tape the joints, creating a

Woodworking Projects

hinge. Be sure that the sharp edges of the bevels come together as cleanly as possible when you apply the tape.

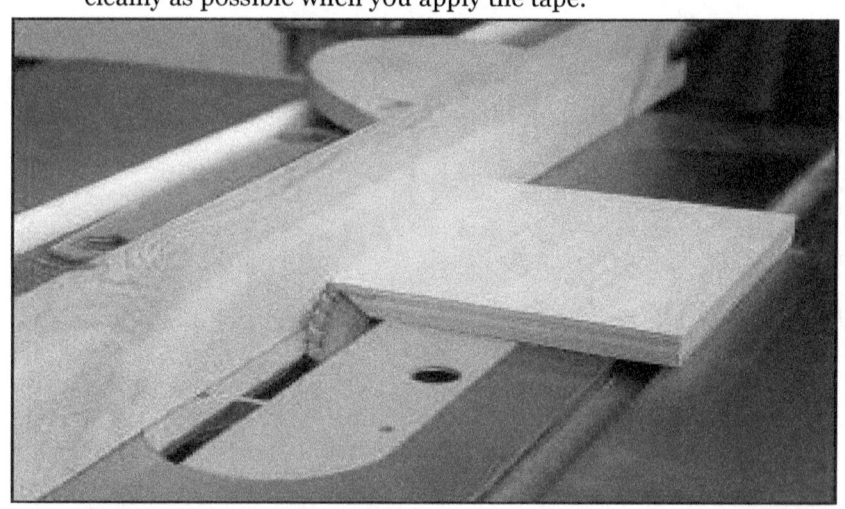

STEP 4:

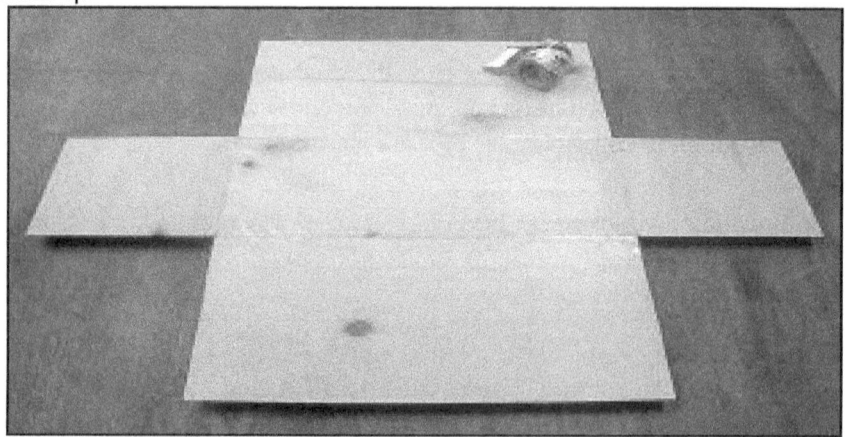

Small Furniture (Beginners Plan)

- Turn the whole assembly face down, then apply glue to all the edges that will be coming together when it's folded up.

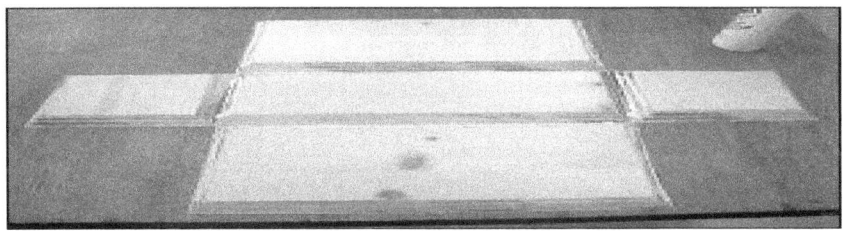

Step 4

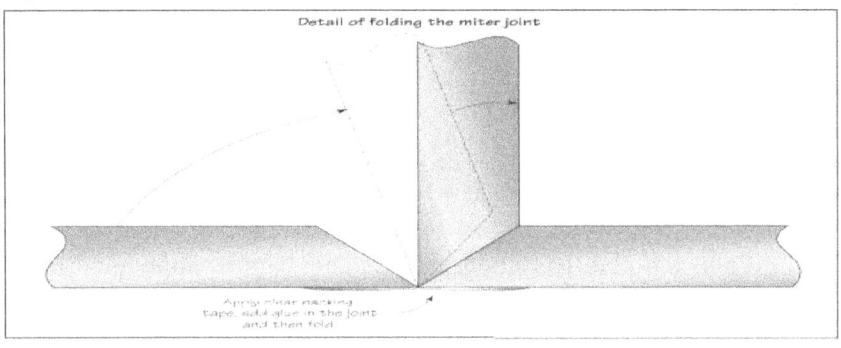

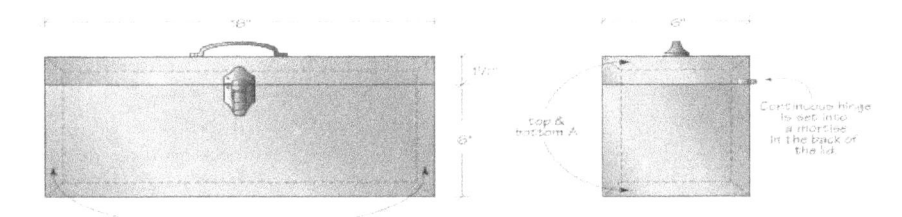

~55~

Woodworking Projects
STEP 5:

- You will need to use a few clamps to hold the side joints tightly. Don't use too much pressure, as that will distort the joint and cause it to open up at the sharp edges.

STEP 6:

- When the glue has dried, remove the clamps, apply glue to the remaining beveled edges, and attach the top.

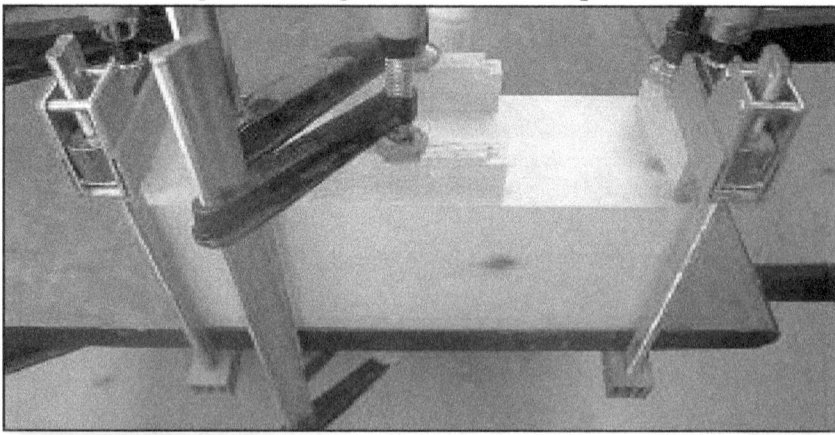

Small Furniture (Beginners Plan)

STEP 7:
- Use blocks under the clamps to even out the pressure. At this point you might be wondering if you could tape the top to the assembly when all the parts are lying flat in Step 3. Yes, you could!

Woodworking Projects

STEP 8:

- When the glue has dried, gently scrape or sand away any glue squeeze-out. Cut the lid off the box, using the table saw.

STEP 9:

- The lid will fit perfectly on the box using this technique.

STEP 10:

- Measure the thickness of the continuous hinge. Set the table saw fence to this measurement and make a through-cut.

STEP 11:

- Reset the fence to the width of the hinge leaf (this does not include the barrel of the hinge) and make the cleanup cut. This cut squares out the corner of the rabbet cut.

Small Furniture (Beginners Plan)

STEP 12:
- Install the hinge. If your cut is accurate, the hinge is lined up easily by holding the edge of the hinge leaf against the shoulder of the rabbet. By allowing the barrel of the hinge to extend beyond the edge of the box, the lid can be opened 180°.

STEP 13:
- This is a quick but neat and tidy way to install a hinge. You can now install the draw bolt and screen door handle.

STEP 14:
- When you've finished the box, the corners will have a nice, clean look. This is a strong joint. The gluing surface is large, and no splines or biscuits are needed.

# GARDEN FURNITURE WITH WOOD PALLETS (BEGINNERS PLAN)

### 1. Pallet Garden Sofa

You can design a sofa with the pallet to decorate your patio and garden area. There are a few tips to design pallet sofa:

**Materials and Tools:**
- 9 Pallets
- Drill, Level, and Hammer
- Sandpaper
- Saw and Nails
- Paint and Paintbrush
- Wood screws

**Steps:**

STEP 1: Collect Your Pallet

The average size of pallet will be 9 and you should select the best quality pallets to design sofa. You can find some cool wood burned or stamped wood. It is important to check a few extra details.

STEP 2: Cut Pallets

You have to cut these pallets at 27.5 inches wide to mix and match them easily. You can cut right directly across the planks and remove a few edges on the side 2 by 4. You can reuse 2 by 4 by sliding it into the space and reattach with the help of nails. The overall length can be 78"x 78".

STEP 3: Create Cushions

You have to hide front 2 by 4 gap of the pallet with cushions and mattresses. You can use a few mattresses to create your own cushion because the foam can be expensive and you can cut an old mattress to make cushions.

STEP 4: Secure Backs

You can use a few screws to overlap pallets and screw them along the seam. It will be good to use 2-inch screws. You can decorate your patio and use in parties for extra sitting arrangements.

2. **Shelves for Garden**
**Materials and Tools:**
- Sandpaper
- Drill, Level, and Hammer
- 2 wood pallets
- Wood screws
- Wood, 2 by 4 inches
- Saw and Nails
- Paint and Paintbrush
- Wall anchors

**Steps:**

STEP 1: In the first step, you have to sand the surface of the wood to get smooth surface pallets. You can use the underside of each pallet.

STEP 2: Wood screws and drills will be used to attach the pallets to each other. Keep one pallet on the top of the each pallet in the same direction. The undersides will grasp the shelves.

STEP 3: Gauge the interior of the top pallet for width and cut the wood in the size of 2 by 4 inches. Insert this wood in the horizontal direction into the pallet and keep it 6 to 8 inches from the top of the wood. Check the level of the wood to make sure it is even before keeping it on the top of the

# Woodworking Projects

wood. Secure the shelf with the use of hammer and nails. Repeat the same process for every shelf.

STEP 4: You can paint your shelves or leave them unfinished to get a rustic look. With the help of wall studs or anchors, you can fix the shelving unit into the wall.

## 3. DIY Garden Chair
**Materials and Tools:**

- Miter saw
- Flat bar
- 2 wooden pallets
- Nail puller
- Box, stainless steel screws
- Measurement tape
- Screw gun

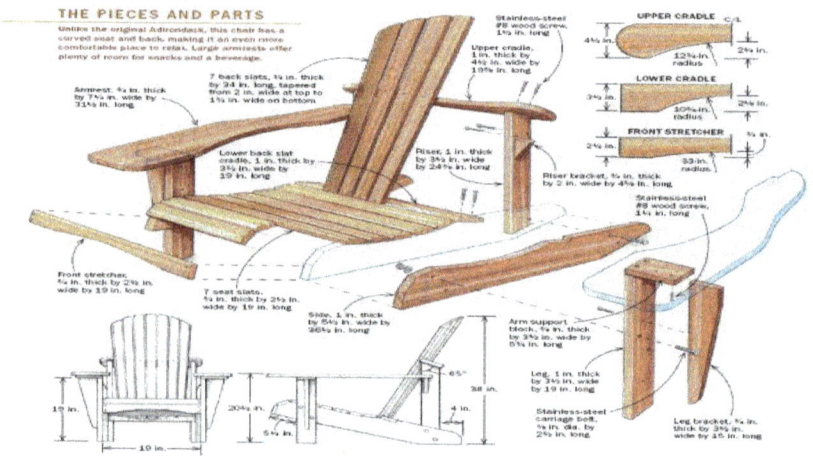

**Steps:**

STEP 1: Take a wooden pallet and keep it flat on the work surface with the peak surface facing up. The flat bar will slide under the first two boards at one end of the pallet and snoop them carefully.

STEP 2: Pull out the nails of every pallet board with the help of nail puller. Clean the pallets by removing any drifted nails and set the boards on one side. Repeat this process and remove the nails from each board and cut the pallet boards for the back of the chair, legs and arms.

STEP 3: Take two boards and measure the 12-inch surface with the help of measure tape and pencil. Use miter saw and cut to the length of the front leg.

STEP 4: Place the end, conflicting the detached boards, on the chair assembly pallet and move it in an upward direction. Keep one forward-facing support on each side at the elevated end and drive four wood screws with equal space through the leg into the exterior of the pallet with the use of screw gun.

STEP 5: Put the second pallet level on the surface while keeping the top surface in an upward direction. Remove half board from one end of the pallet and clean it by pulling the nails out with the help of nail puller. This pallet will help you to assemble seat and ends with the removal of boards for back legs.

STEP 6: Insert the pallet designed for a back seat with the back leg down through the fourth board. Bring down the back legs on the work surface and used four screws to fasten the seat. You can use a screw gun to fix the each joint of the chair.

4. **DIY Coffee Table**
**Materials and Tools:**
- Drill
- Hot glue gun
- Paint or stain
- Chest or suitcase
- Staple gun
- Measuring tape
- Legs and Storage containers
- Top plate hardware
- Velvet or fabric
- Wallpaper
- Cording or trim

Woodworking Projects

- Wooden divide

**Steps:**
STEP 1: Sand the pallet woods and then paint them to complement the colors of your chest. Carefully examine the chest and remove any torn fabric to give a neat look to your coffee table storage.

STEP 2: Measure the legs and then prepare all four legs to secure them at a right place. You can use a machine gun to fix nails and use wooden dividers to make small compartments. It will be good to decorate your wooden dividers with wallpaper.

### 5. Pallet Stool for Garden
**Materials and Tools:**
- 4 pieces of wood to make the legs of the stool (3 inches thick)
- Drill and wood glue
- 4 inch thick wood for seat
- Chisel
- 4 large screws
- Varnish
- Padding and upholstery

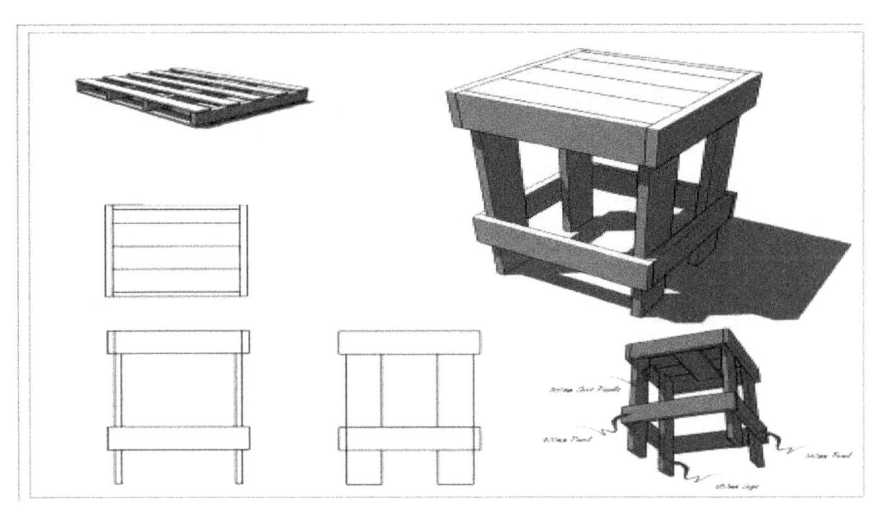

**Steps:**
STEP 1: Measure the stool as per your needs and then select pallet wood to make the stool. Cut into different pieces of the wood to make legs and seat. The seat can be round or square.

STEP 2: Drill holes in the seat to fix legs in the four corners, you need to insert screws into each of the four corners on the bar stool. Cut down the legs to determine the height of your stool and try to keep these pieces 3 inches thick. Make sure to keep the size of all four legs same.

STEP 3: You can use wood glue in the holes of the seat around the screw head and carefully insert the legs into the hole. Screw them until you get resistance and make sure to keep it tight. Clean the excessive glue and let the stool dry.

Woodworking Projects

# PLANTERS; SHEDS; AND PLAYHOUSE (BEGINNERS PLAN)

1. **Playhouse in Patio**

**Materials and Tools:**

- 1 sheet 1/2-inch pallet wood, 8 feet x 4 feet
- Circular saw and Hammer
- Tape measure
- Straight edge
- 2-inch galvanized nails
- Pencil
- Construction adhesive
- 21 x 34 inches for bottom
- 27 x 39 inches for top
- 23 x 24 inches for back
- 23 x 24 inches for front
- 24 x 34 inches for side
- 24 x 34 inches for another side

**Steps:**
STEP 1: Cut the pieces of pallet wood boards for the following measurements:
STEP 2: You have to create a door at the bottom edge of the front piece, but mark it with a pencil. You can cut out the rectangle or round door.

STEP 3: Line up the back panel and the panels on both the sides and fix with nail and hammer along the length of the panels. Now secure the front panel with hammering electrified nails.

STEP 4: It is time to set the wooden frame on the top of the bottom piece and fix it with two to three nails on each corner. Keep a flat panel in its place with hammer and nails and keep it secure. Add adhesive constructions and let the pet house dry.

## 2. Rack to Keep Your Tools

**Materials and Tools:**
- 1 pallet
- Staples
- 4' x 4' chicken wire
- 6 wire coat hangers
- Durable chain
- 2 1/4 x 4" clasp hook bolts and nuts
- 4 washers with bolts
- S-shaped hooks

Woodworking Projects

- Circular Saw and Hammer
- Nail Puller and Nails
- Drill and head screwdriver
- Staple gun and wire cutters
- Tape to Measure

**Steps:**

STEP 1: Cut the pallets and remove the middle bar of the pallet. Carefully split the wood and measure the split pieces. You should use a staple gun to staple the chicken wire in a particular place. Staple the chicken wire to the wooden bar.

STEP 2: Cut the additional wire with the help of a wire cutter and bend the remaining wire to make the sharp corners smooth. Take the wooden bars and fix the chicken wire with the help of screws and use a nail gun to fix the wood pallets.

STEP 3: Fix the chain along the length and hang the rack at about a 45-degree angle with hook bolts on the wall. Your pot rack is ready and now you can use bolts to fix the rack at a point where you can access it and create additional support.

STEP 4: You can place S-hooks on the hanger wire so that you can hang pots and pans on the hooks. Keep it in mind that these hooks can carry a lightweight item, but you can get the benefits of additional storage.

3. **Pallet Bin for Compost and Plants**

**Materials and Tools:**

- 8-foot pieces of 1 x 4 pine, 2 boards
- 10-foot pieces of 1 x 2 pine, 2 boards
- 10-foot piece of 2 x 2 pine, 1 board

- Measuring tape and Clamp
- Safety goggles
- Circular saw
- 1 box of about 1 1/4-inch screws
- Drill and 7/16 drill bit

**Steps:**
STEP 1: Cut all the wooden pieces with the help of a circular saw, such as you need 4 pieces of 24-inch of 1 x 4, 4 pieces of 22 inches, and 4 pieces of 2 x 2 at 30 inches. You will also cut 4 pieces of 1 x 2 at 24 inches and 6 pieces of 25 inches.

STEP 2: You need to build four walls, two walls will be built by 22-inch piece of 1 x 4 and two walls can be designed with 24-inch one x four pieces. You will make square walls build the corners. Fasten them together and assemble the top and bottom area.

STEP 3: Cut the sections for inner rack and drill a screw in each rack to fix it. Finish off the bottom part and prepare the top part in the same way. You can add sealant or paint to protect the rack.

## 4. Grow Your Herbal Garden

**Materials and Tools:**
- Wall adhesive
- Tapcon screws
- Wooden pallet
- Hose clamps
- Mason jars
- Soil
- Cable Staples

Woodworking Projects

- Charcoal
- Stones
- Plants

**Steps:**

STEP 1: Use a wood that will serve as a base for the wall and place hose clamps on this wooden board. You can measure the place on a wooden board to find out the capacity of glass jars on the wooden board. If you want to grow herbs, these should be located close to your window. You can grow sage, rosemary, and similar herbs.

STEP 2: After securing the boards in its place, you can use adhesive to secure the board and use tap con screw to make it secure in its place. Now you will measure the center to fix the hose clamps and secure them in their right place.

STEP 3: Pour stones in the bottom of mason jars and make sure these should be free from drainage. After stones, you can add charcoal to balance the pH of soil and avoid growth of bacteria in soil. Now add soil and plants in every jar and secure them with the hose clamps.

**5. Storage Shed for Garden**
**Materials and Tools:**

- Tape Measure
- 1 board of 24 feet, 2 x 4 inch
- Flour
- Jig saw

- Rubber mallet
- 6 Reber of 4 foot
- Hammer
- 3 lengths of 14 PVC pipe, ¾ inch and 12 feet long
- Polyethylene 12 x 2 feet plastic
- Nails
- Fencing staples
- Wire

**Steps:**
STEP 1: Gauge the footprint of your transferable garage. You have to mark this particular area with flour. The garage should be 6' long and 4' wide.

STEP 2: You can hammer the supports of Rebar halfway into the floor at each corner of the garage along with the rubber mallet. Now hammer the leftover supports into the ground halfway on every side of the shed.

STEP 3: Curve every piece of the PVC to make a U-shape and keep arm of every U at the end of Rebar support gluing out of the floor.

STEP 4: Now drape a wire all the way around the bend of the first segment of PVC pipe. Now, loosely run a wire to the 2nd segment of pipe and drape it. You can expand the wire to the last segment of pipe and drape it loosely. You can create a ridge post that will be good to bear the weight of snow.

STEP 5: Now cut the board into two pieces of 6-foot and one piece of 4-foot. You need additional wood to make an open square. You can keep this square at the bottom of the garage frame outer surface of the Rebar and leave a single side open.

STEP 6: It is time to pull the polyethylene shell at the peak of the garage border to keep one side flush to the façade of the garage. You can nail it down with the fencing tacks. It is time to leave a back lynching loose so that the wind can escape out from the front to the back and the rain will not come as well.

# GARDEN BENCH AND CHAIRS (INTERMEDIATE PLAN)

## 1. Garden Bench

### Materials and Tools
- 5 pieces of lumber (2 x 4 x 8 ft)
- 1 piece of lumber (1 x 4 x 4 ft)
- 1 piece of lumber (4 x 4 x 8 ft)
- 2 threaded rod (3/8-in.-dia x 36-in.)
- 4 of each hex nuts and washers (3/8-in.). The outside diameter should be 9/16 in.
- Polyurethane glue
- 1 wooden dowel (1-in.-dia.)
- 1 box decking screws (1 5/8-in.)
- 1 box galvanized finishing nails (1 1/2-in. (4d))

### Steps:

STEP 1: Use a circular/power mister saw and a crosscut guide then cut 4 legs, 12 spacers to length and 9 seat boards. Use a table saw to cut the tenon into the top of each leg. Make shoulder cuts into opposite sides of each leg and clamp a small stop block rip fence. Adjust the outside blade to be 3½ inches from the stop block. Set the blade to 1 3/8 inches high then butt the leg against the stop block and use a miter gauge to push it across the blade.

STEP 2: Start to flip the legs over then make a second shoulder cut. While holding the leg against the miter gauge move the fence to the side and repeatedly make passes over the blade to remove bulk of each tenon. Pare to perfection by the use of a razor-sharp chisel.

STEP 3: Pin to six 2in × 4in seat panels blocks 3 ½ inches square and ¾ inches thick as insertions. By the use of a 1 ½ inch 4 diameter finishing nails and glue fasten the block with outer edge on ends.

STEP 4: To fasten a leg at each end of 2 seat boards that don't have spacers attached use the glue and 1 5/8-inch galvanized decking screws. on the 2 outer seat boards for the counter bored holes mark center points for the rods and nuts that hold the seat together. Now, drill a ¾-inch- hole with 1-inch-diameter. The wood plug will be received by the counter bored holes and they will eliminate the hex nuts on the ends of the rods that are threaded.

STEP 5: Make a plywood dance and screw it onto a guide for you to be able to drill the 7/16-inch-diameter holes for the rods. This will make sure that any hole complete each piece is precisely located relative to the panel's end. Then try to hold the jig to be alongside the end of each seat panel before boring through the panel and spacer block.

STEP 6: On a workbench glue and clamp all the fragments together and cut the threaded pole to have a measurement of nineteen inches. Onto the end of each rod thread a nut, eliminate the nut for you to clean up any saw damage.

STEP 7: Place a nut and washer at the ends of each pole then with a 9/16-inch socket ratchet it fitted.

STEP 8: Into each whole glue a rod plug and cut it flush to the face of the seat board.

STEP 9: Use 80- or 100-grit sandpaper to respectively even surfaces then use a clean brush to remove any sanding dust. Apply a clear wood preservative to provide adequate protection for the wood. Brush off fallen leaves that may stain it and store the bench indoors in winter.

Woodworking Projects

## 2. Camp Kitchen
## Materials and Tools:

| |
|---|
| 1 Bottom -- 32-1/2" x 14 x 1/2" |
| 2 Sides --19" x 14" x 1/2" |
| 1 Divider -- 18- 1/2" x 14" x 1/2" |
| 1 Shelf -- 20" x 14 x1/2" |
| 1 Top -- 12" x 14" x 1/2" |
| 1 Top Leaf, Right -- 12-1/2" x 14-1/4" x1/2" |
| 1 Top Leaf, Left – 20-7/8" x 14-1/4" x1/2" |
| 1 Door, Left –12 ¾"x 20" x ½" |
| 1 Door, Right --18"x12"x ½" |
| 1 Back – ¾"- ½"" x 19" x ¼" |
| Base (made of hardwood) |
| 2 pieces 31-1/2" x 3/4" |
| 2 Pieces -- 12" x 3/4" |
| 4 Legs -- 1" x 1" x12" |
| 2 Pieces Stop Molding 3/4" x3/8" for Door Stops |
| Hardware |
| 4 Pairs, butt hinges 1" x 2" or piano hinge |
| 2 Door knobs |
| 2 Roller Catches |
| 2 Folding Trays for the Top Leafs |
| 1/4 lb. 1- 1/2" finishing nails |
| Glue |
| 4 Carriage Bolts complete with Washers and Wing Nuts -- 2" x 1/4" |
| 1 Pint Marine or Outdoor Quality Paint |

**Steps:**
1) You will need approximately 1 sheet of 4' x 8' x 1/2 "plywood (no more).
2) Cut all pieces to the sizes given on your material list.
3) Using glue on every joint, begin by nailing both sides against the ends of the bottom.
4) Next measure 5-1/4" down from the top on both your left side and the divider and nail the shelf in place, the top (right) comes next and the divider is then nailed onto the bottom.
5) Every piece must be square-cut, of course, and, with the back glued and nailed will stiffen the whole cabinet.
6) Doors and top leafs are fitted next and, using either butt or piano hinges, screwed into place.

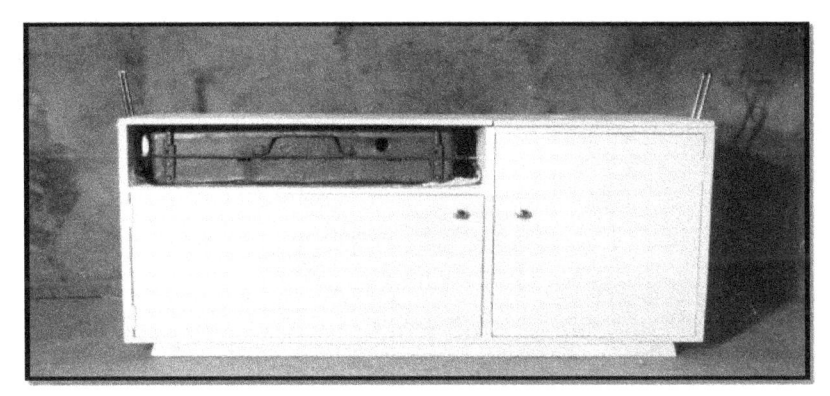

7) Stop molding is nailed to the divider and roller catches fastened to them to hold the doors secure. Install door knobs and leaf stays last.
8) Both leafs must be mortised to accept the stays when the top is open. Take care to install the stays so that the leafs stand out square to the cabinet sides.
9) The interior arrangement is subject to personal preference and should be made to accept your existing gear.
10) See the model photo #1 below
11) The small divider on the right side must be large enough to accept a gasoline can.
12) A camp lantern, either single or double burner, will fit next to it and is held in place by 2 screw eyes or hooks and a rubber band to prevent it from rattling.
13) On the left an extra shelf can be installed to accept camp griddle or other miscellaneous items.
14) A dishpan with nesting cook and dinnerware is held in place by a small wooden molding and again hooks and rubber band.
15) Cutlery, openers etc., will fit into another small divider.

Woodworking Projects

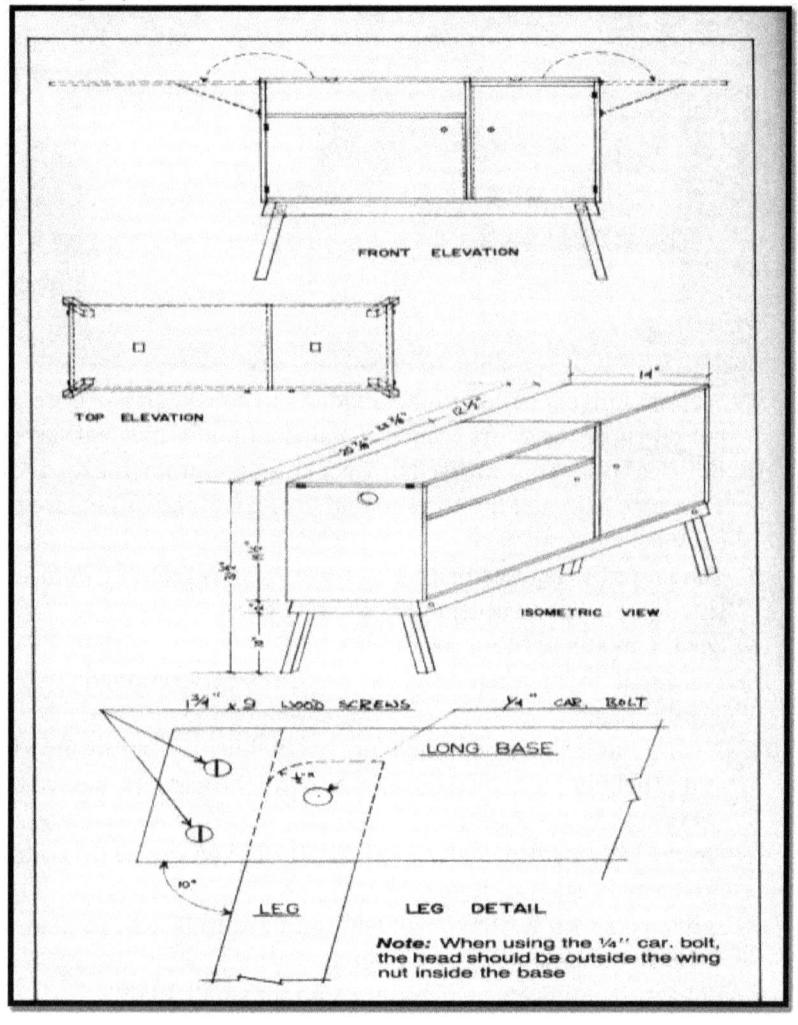

16) The base is cut from hardwood and can be glued and nailed, with the end pieces fitting between the long pieces.
17) The legs are bolted, one bolt to each leg, but care must be taken that they will fold completely inside the base and when you are folding them out. They must be close enough to the outside of the base so that they cannot fold out further than about 10 degrees.
18) The wing nuts will allow you to tighten the bolts so that the legs cannot fold accidently but are still somewhat adjustable.

3. **Adirondack Chair**

This is the least demanding to assemble and sturdiest Adirondack seat that you can make. We made the base more grounded with all 2x4 encircling. This Adirondack seat is a peruser most loved and has been assembled a large number of times.

**Materials:**
- 3 – 2×4 @ 8 feet long
- 1 – 2×2 @ 6 feet long
- 4 – 1×4 @ 8 feet long
- (30) 2 1/2" self-tapping wood screws

- (60) 2" self-tapping wood screws
- (20) 1 1/4" wood screws
- exterior appropriate wood glue

**Cut List**

- 2 - 2x4 @ 20 3/4" long with both ends cut parallel at 15 degrees o square (back legs)
- 2 - 2x4 @ 20" (front legs)
- 2 - 2x2 @ 26 1/2" long, longest point measurement, one end cut at 15 degrees o square (arm support)
- 2 - 2x4 @ 31 7/8" long, one end cut at 35 degrees o square to longest point, other end cut at 20 degrees o square to shortest point - see step 1 (stringers)
- 2 - 2x4 @ 22 1/2" (front apron and back support)
- 5 - 1x4 @ 22 1/2" (seat slats)
- 5 - 1x4 @ 36" (back slats)
- 1 - 1x4 @ 19 1/2" (back top support)
- 1 - 2x4 @ 19 1/2" (back base support)
- 2 - 1x4 @ 27" (arm rests)

**Tools**

- Tape Measure
- Safety Glasses
- Jigsaw
- Speed Square
- Ear Protection
- Miter saw
- Pencil
- Drill
- Sander

**Steps:**

STEP 1: Cut 2- 2x 4s 31 7/8" long, with one end cut at 35 degrees off four-sided, and other end cut at 20 degrees off four-sided. The cuts are not parallel because they have different degrees, but are cut in the same direction. Then take the 20 degrees off square side and mark at a 90 degree angle with a square 2" across and cut off with a circular saw or jigsaw.

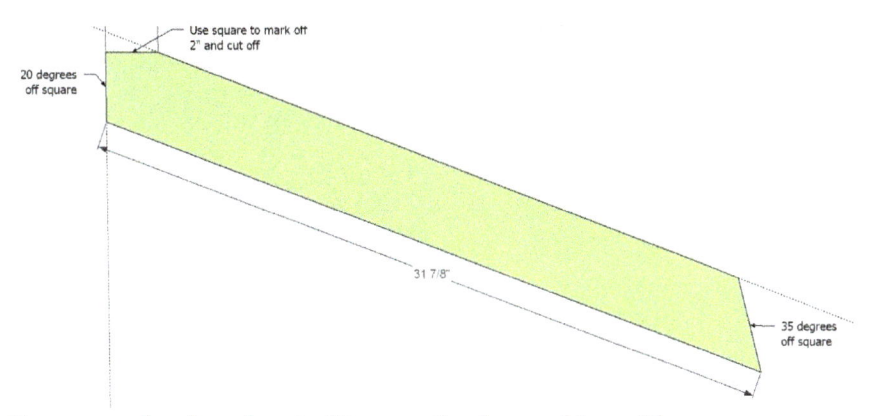

From stretcher board, cut off top portion by marking with a square and cutting off with a jigsaw. Do this on both stretcher boards.

STEP 2:

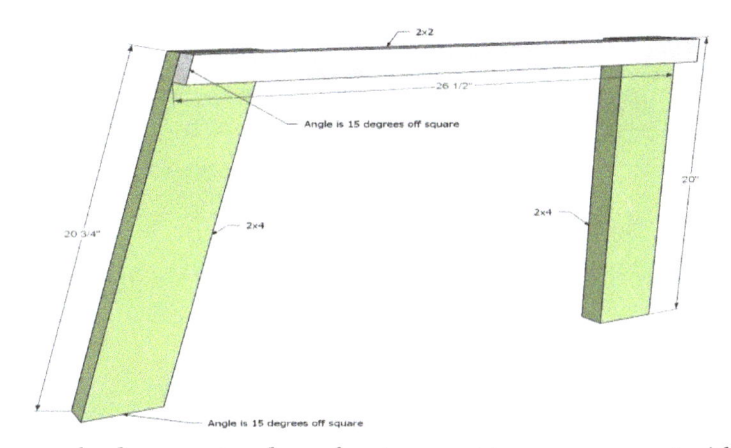

Fasten one back support and one front support to a arm support with 2 1/2" exterior screws. Keep the top and outside edges flush.

STEP 3:

Woodworking Projects

*Note that 2x2 arm support is now on outside*

*2 1/2" exterior screws and glue*

*1/2*

*2 1/2" screws*

*13 3/4"*

*35 degrees off square*

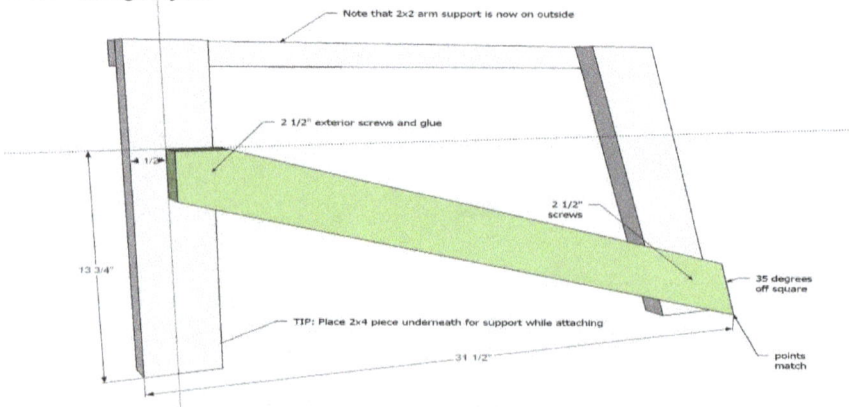

*TIP: Place 2x4 piece underneath for support while attaching*

*31 1/2"*

*points match*

STEP 4:

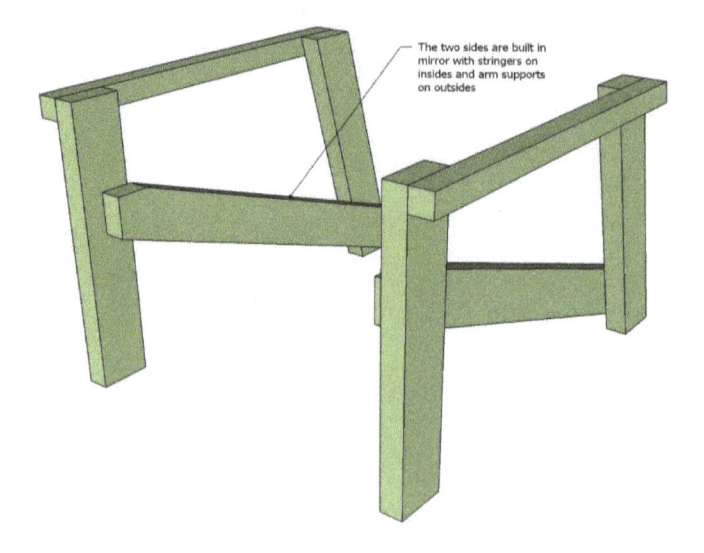

*The two sides are built in mirror with stringers on insides and arm supports on outsides*

Build opposite side of chair in mirror, with arm supports to outside and stretcher to inside. Make sure the two match up.

STEP 5

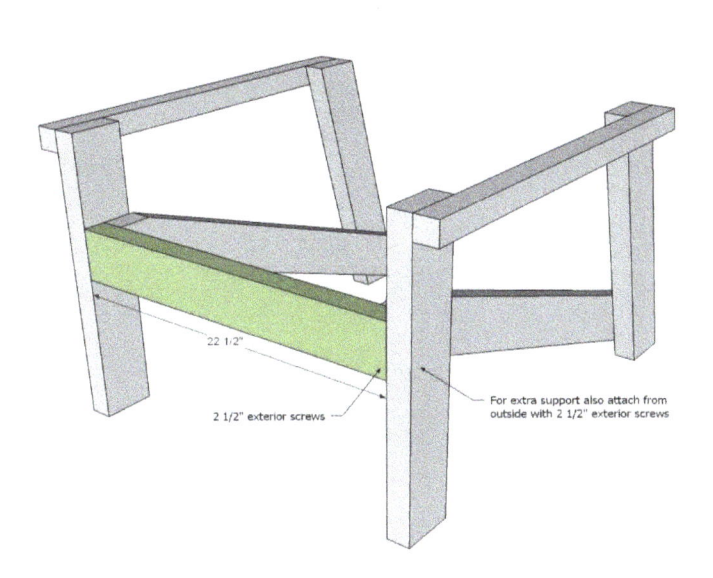

Visible Bib is attached to facades of stretcher and from outside of chair for added support.

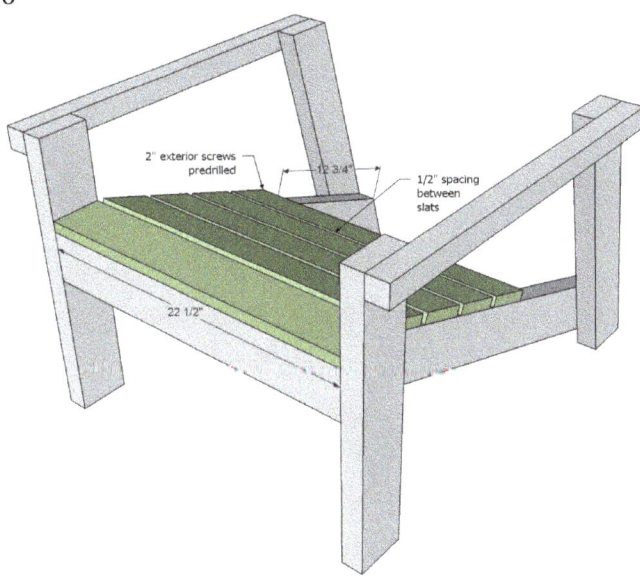

STEP 6

Start at the anterior of the chair and attach chair planks to stretcher with 2" screws and glue. Leave a 1/2" opening between chair slats.

Woodworking Projects
## STEP 7

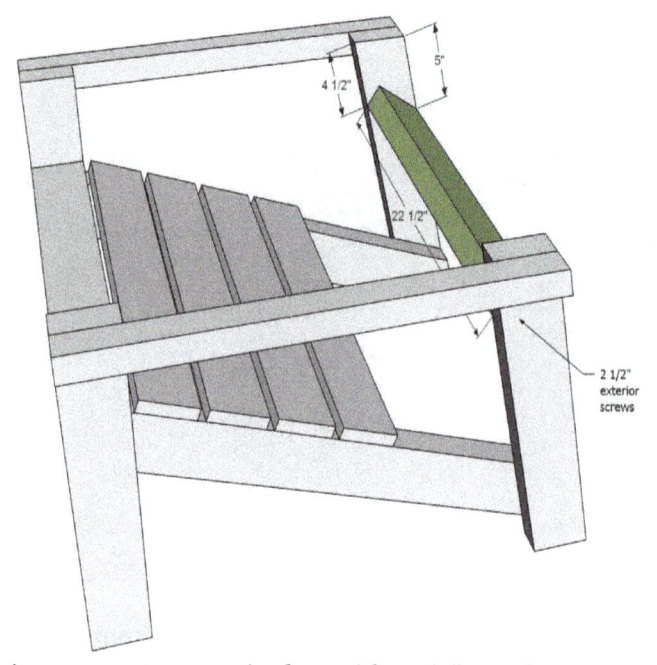

Attach posterior support to posterior legs with 2 1/2" exterior screws, corresponding up dimensions in illustrations.
## STEP 8

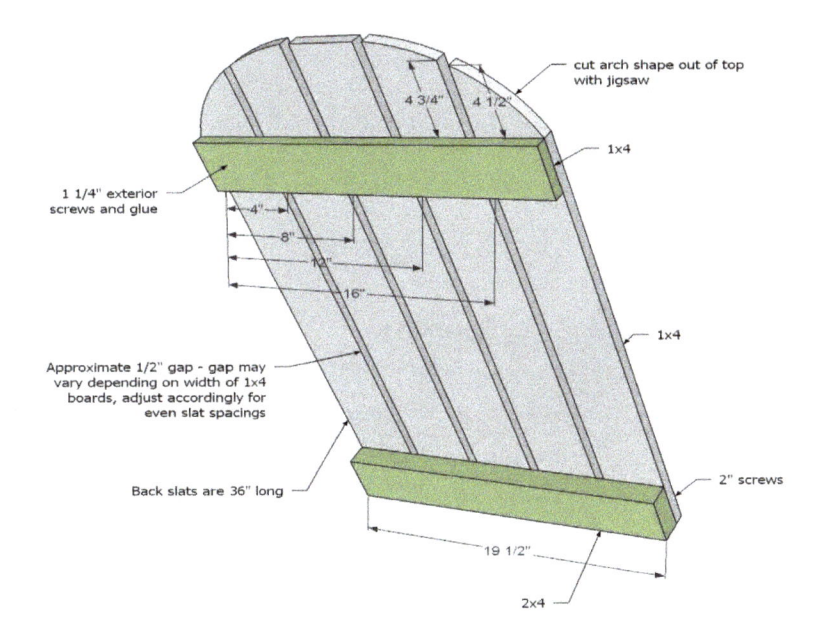

Build back by fastening all back panels to chair back base support,

Leaving almost 1/2" gap in between. Then fasten at top with screws. Cut arch shape on back top.
STEP 9

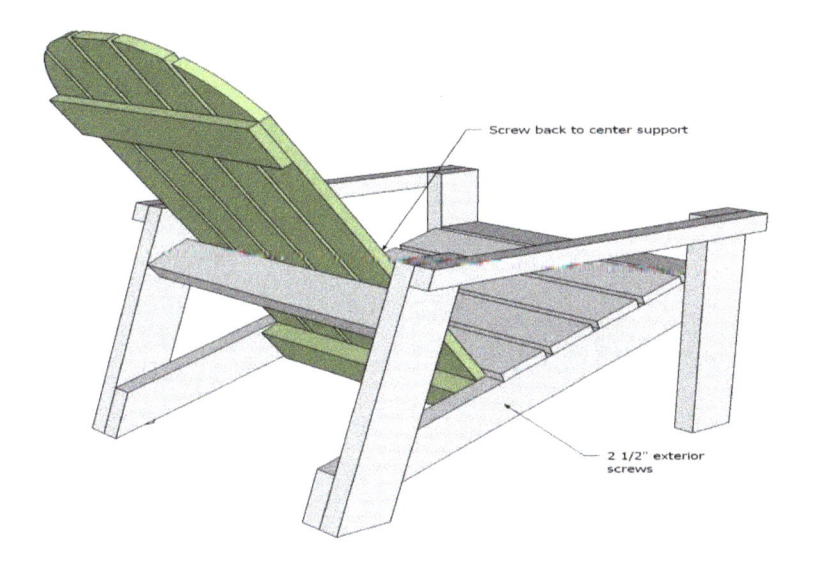

Woodworking Projects

Place posterior inside chair and safe in place with 2 1/2" exterior screws. Also fasten back to back support with 2" exterior screws.

STEP 10

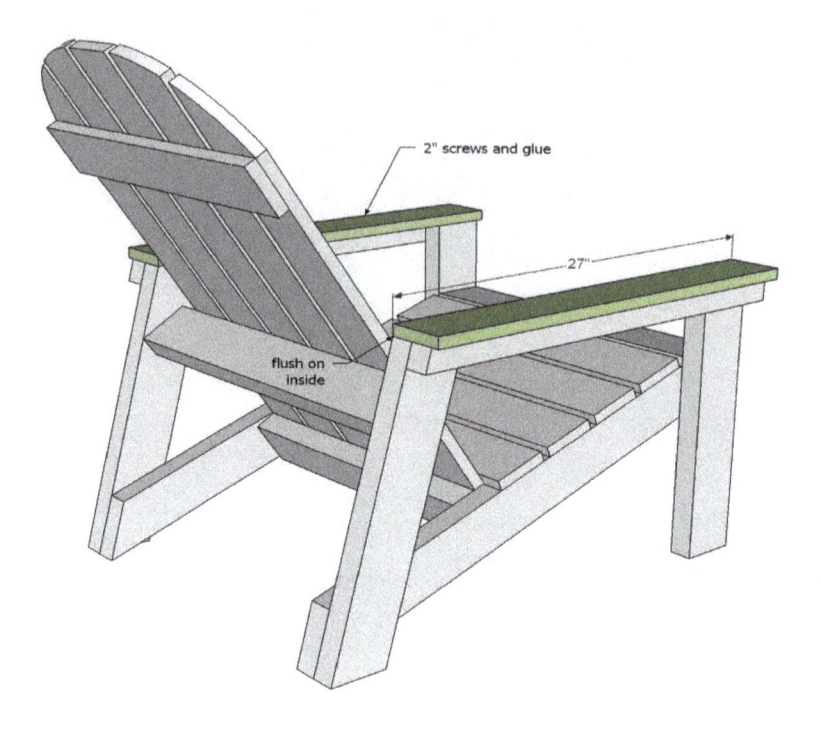

Secure armrests to arm support and tops of legs with screws and glue.
STEP 11

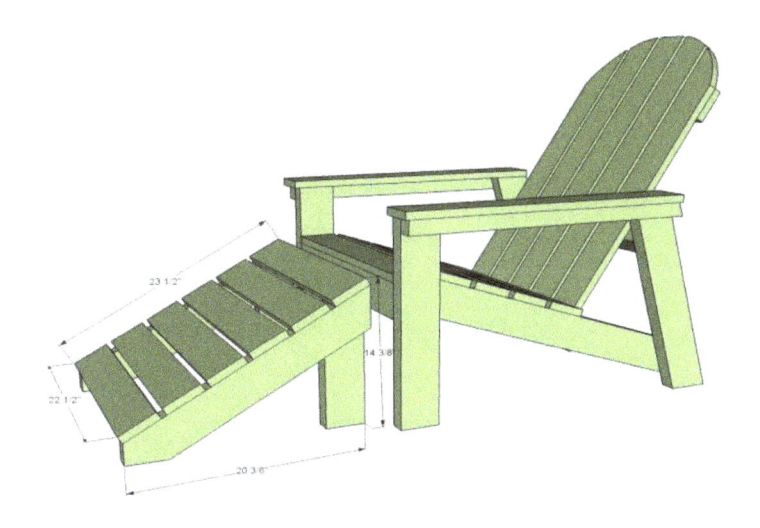

Optional Adirondack Footstool Plans

Adding a footrest to your Adirondack chair will increase the coziness! We've included the plans below that match this Adirondack plan.

**Footstool Shopping List**

1 - 2x4 @ 8 feet long or stud length

1 - 1x4 @ 12 feet long

2" and 2 1/2" exterior screws

**Footstool Cut List**

2 - 2x4 @ 23 1/2" long with both ends cut at 30 degrees off square, equivalent to each other, long point to short point dimension (stringers)

5 - 1x4 @ 22 1/2" (top boards)

2 - 2x4 @ 13 3/4" long with one end cut at 30 degrees off four-sided, longest point dimension (legs)

Woodworking Projects
## STEP 12

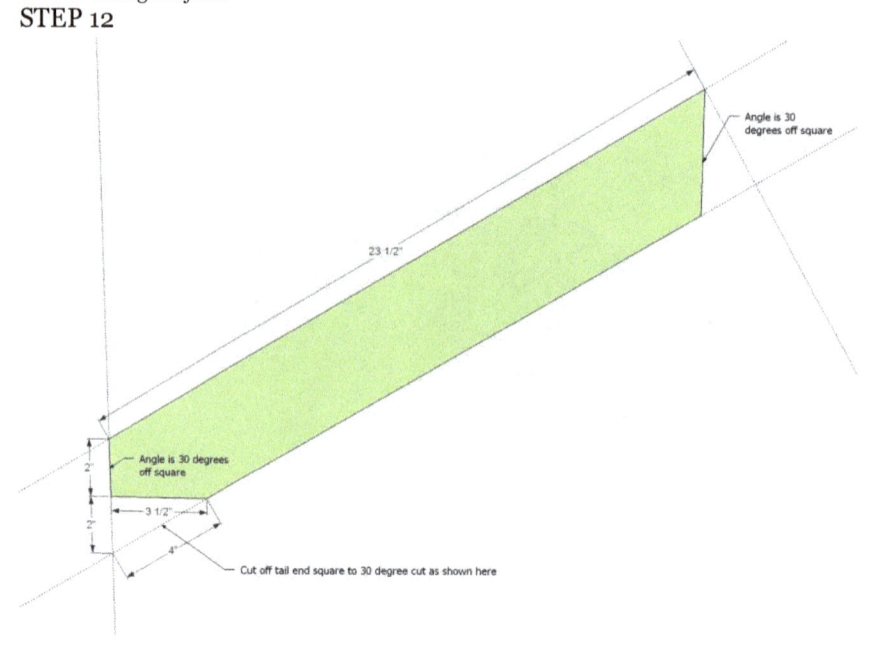

Cut the Adirondack footrest stringers with a complex miter saw first. Then use a square to spot the cut off and cut with jigsaw or circular saw.

## STEP 13

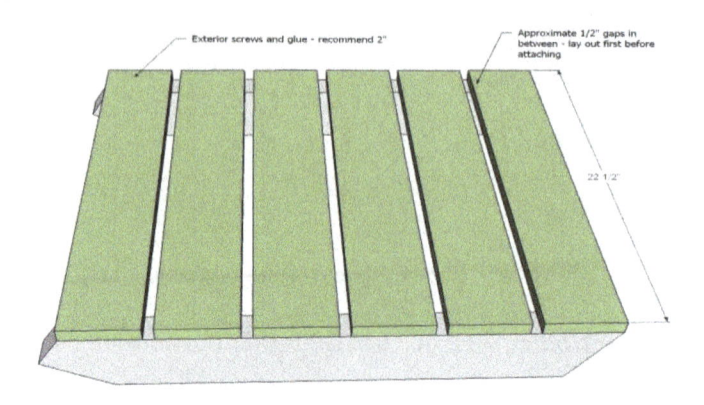

Use 2" fastens and adhesive to attach the deck panels on top of the stringers.

STEP 14

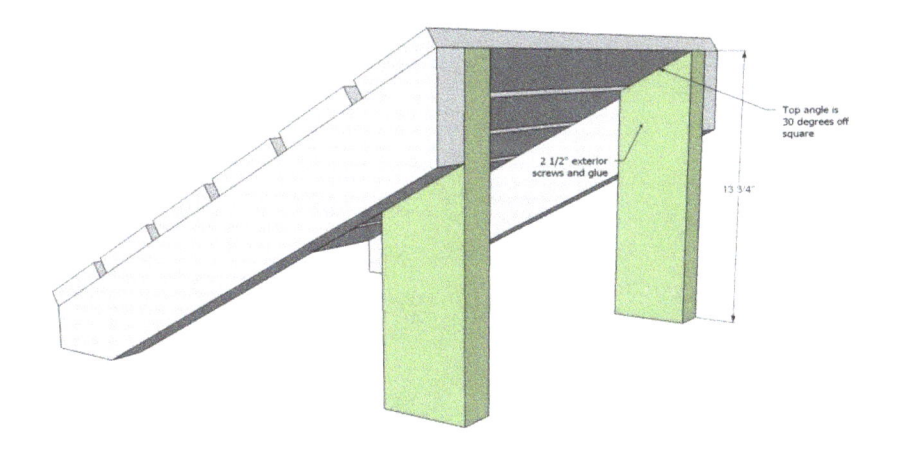

Attach supports with 2-1/2" screws to insides of the stringers to complete

The footstool.

**Finishing Instructions**

Seal all holes with wood filler and let dry. Apply extra coats of wood filler as desired. After the wood filler is totally dry, smoothen the finished project in the track of the wood grain with sandpaper. Remove sanding dust. Remove all sanding dust on work planes as well. Wipe project clean with moist cloth. It is always suggested to apply a test coat on a hidden area or scrap piece to guarantee color evenness and bond. Use primer or wood conditioner as desired.

Woodworking Projects

# "MARSH FOX" DUCK PUNT (ADVANCE PLAN)

THE MARSH FOX is a one-man duck punt especially designed for the marshes of B.C. but could be used by anyone wanting to access wetlands and barrier islands. It may also be used on small lakes in calm weather. Always err on the side of caution when boating and wear a flotation device.

**Materials:**

| Item | Number of Pieces | Size | Length |
| --- | --- | --- | --- |
| Strong-back | 1 | 2" x 10" | 144" |
| Strong-Back Base | Assorted lumber | 2" x 4" | |
| Planking | 3 | 1/8" x 48" | 96" |
| Transom | 1 | 3/4" x 17" | 24" |
| Frames | 4 | 3/4" x 2-3/4" | 52" |
| Chines Laminate | 4 | 3/8 x 1-1/4" | 150" |
| Sheer Laminate | 4 | 3/8" x 1- 1/4" | 150" |

| | | | |
|---|---|---|---|
| Keel | 1 | 3/4" x 1-1/2" | 144" |
| Skegs (outer keels) | 2 | 7/8" x 2" | 96" |
| Gunwale (outer) | 4 | 1/2" x 3/4" | 150" |
| Bottom Battens | 4 | 3/4" x 1" | 132" |
| Chine (outer) | 2 | 1/2" x 3/4" | 150" |
| Deck Battens | 3 | 3/4" x 1-1/2" | 38" |
| Stem | 2 | 2" x 6" | 14" |
| Transom knee laminate | 2 | 3/4" x 15" | 15" |
| Floor board | 1 | 1/2" x 33" | 82" |
| Splash rail (coaming) | 2 | 1/2" x 4 - 3/4" | 96" |
| Splash rail (coaming) | 1 | 1/2" x 4 - 3/4" | 120" |
| Woodscrews | 1/2 gross | 1-1/2" x8 | |
| Anchor fast nails | 2 pounds | | 5/8 " |
| Glue | 2 -1/2 pounds | | |
| Eye Bolts | 1 | 1/4" | 5" |
| Eye Bolts | 2 | 1/4" | 2" |
| Seam or Bedding Compound | 1 - 1/2 lbs. | | |
| Paint | 1/2-gallon flat gray | | |
| Paint | 3 camouflage colors | | |
| Fiberglass (Cloth) | Medium Weight | 44" x 144" | can be cut |
| Resin (all purpose) | 1/2 gallon | complete with | hardeners |
| Acetone solvent | 1/4 gallon for | brush cleaner | |
| Paint thinners | 1/4 gallon | | |
| Bow & Transom Handles | 3 | | |
| Push -pole | 1 | 2"x6" | 10 feet |

Woodworking Projects

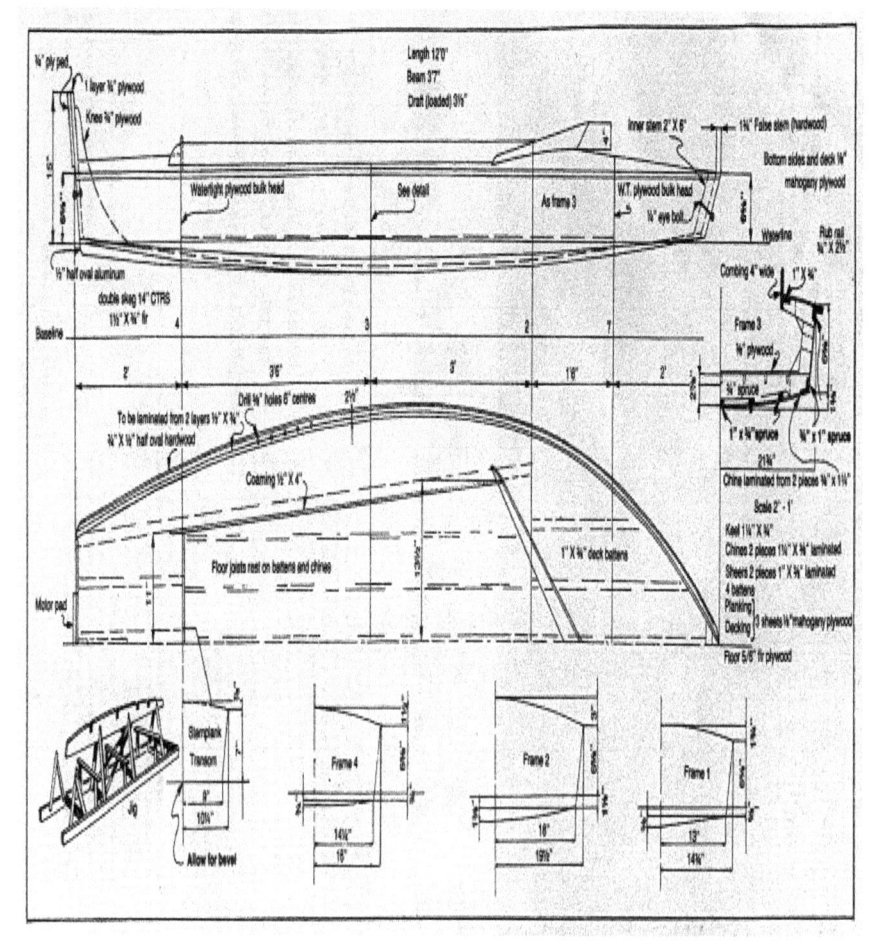

**Steps:**
1. To simplify construction, build the Marsh Fox in the upside-down position on a strong-back jig or form. (see sketch) Special tools or a steam box are not required.
2. Make a full-size layout and begin by transferring all lines and measurements, full size, onto some sheets of plywood or heavy building paper to assure that smooth lines will result.
3. Mark out the keel line, stem and transom angles on a 2" x 10" x12' straight plank, cut and planed into the prescribed shape. Obtain the stem and transom angles from the plan as well. Mark them out on the plank and saw into shape. Plane all saw cuts smooth and fair as this will be your construction strong-back.

4. Use any scrap lumber for bases or legs and frame support bracing. If possible, nail the strong back's legs to the workshop floor but take care to set it up level.
5. Additional braces for the frame are added as required to hold the punt's framework rigid. This is very important as your punt will only be as fair-lined as your jig permits.
6. This jig will allow you to work in a comfortable position and it will keep the punt's assembled frame rigid.
7. Next notch out the strong-back at each frame station and draw a straight center line along its upper edge. This will be the punt's center line as well. Later, you can use the center of the strong back as the centerline for the punt.
8. When making the frames, transom and stem, take all measurements from the full-size layout.
9. Mark the full-size measurements of each frame station on heavy paper or plywood and draw out their lines well. (These are used as checkpoints when the frames are assembled later)
10. Transfer all lines onto the frame lumber and saw out the pieces. Assemble using ¼" (0.6-cm) plywood for connecting corner gussets. These are glued and nailed to the frame pieces.
11. Number 1 and 4 frames are notched out (see detail) to accept the bottom reinforcing battens. Number 2 and 3 are sawn out to allow water such as rain or spray to flow freely about the bilge without rising "frame high" in any one section and thereby upsetting the punt's balance. A tight fit is essential here.
12. Tack all frames into position on the strong-back. Then square them to the center line of the jig and plumb to the waterline of the punt.
13. Next saw out the transom as a 1 piece unit and level the edges to approximately 12 degrees "lean –out" on the bottom and 8 degrees on the sides. (The angles must be checked and be adjusted after battens are installed prior to the installation of the sheeting or planking.) Tack the transom into place.
14. Using a straight-grained, limber batten at least 12 feet (3.6 m) long, mark and align the exact positions of all the battens on the bottom as well as the chines and sheer battens.
15. Notch the transom, stem and frames to receive them.
16. Beginning with the keel, tack it lightly all along the strongback to insure a clean, smooth line. Next, glue and screw the transom, stem and frames (not to strongback) and take care not to splinter the wood.

## Woodworking Projects

17. If necessary, drill screw holes and take care not to split the wood when countersinking the screws. Fasten the battens in the same manner.
18. Before planking can begin, remove all tacks from the keel. The notches for them will then have to be beveled to correspond to the curves of the hull. Also notch the stem and transom, but double-check the bevel angles here.
19. Apply glue to the frame connections, and fasten to the frames, stem and transom (no glue to strong-back).
20. Begin the lamination of the chines & sheer battens by fastening the first layer into the stem notch & then blend this batten along proper lines& fasten this as you proceed.
21. Fit the second layer and start the thin "anchor fast nails" at about 2" intervals. Then apply glue and nail it to the first batten.
22. Use a heavy block of wood for backing and drive these nails in very gently so no drilling will be required.
23. Before planking, plane the appropriate (natural) bevels on all battens and then remove all temporary tacks from the keel.
24. Chines and sheer battens are laminated where circumstances do not permit the steaming of the wood to facilitate easy bending.
25. When laminating, begin by fastening the half-sized stringer to the stem notch, gently draping it around (and fastening as you go) all frame stations and to the transom.
26. Before cutting to exact lengths always double check because the transom does lean out.
27. Then apply glue and fit the second layer of wood, nailing it gently to the first. Do not place nails where bevels have to be planed.
28. Use a back-up heavy block of wood when nailing. Some areas may require drilled pilot holes to prevent splitting.
29. After the glue has set (overnight) plane or correct all bevels so the planking material will have a maximum glue surface.
30. To avoid waste, make a plank pattern out of plywood strips or heavy building paper and drape it over the area to be sheeted in.
31. If 8' (2.4-m) plywood sheets are used, care must be taken that not all butt joints are in the same location around the hull.
32. All butt joints should be backed by plywood blocks that are fitted and glued tightly between the battens.
33. The planking completed, lift the hull off the "jig" which can now be discarded.
34. Cut out and install the transom knee and the bulkheads (if desired), also the outside stem shoe.

35. Then install all eyebolts, deck beams, the deck battens and paint the inside of the hull.
36. N.B. If foam is to be installed, do not paint at this stage.
37. Next, a ¾" (1.8-cm) plumb face is planed around the gunwales and the rubrail is laminated around the hull.
38. When the glue has set -- drill a number of 5/8" (1.3-cm) holes into the rail. Lean the drill somewhat at an angle (from the center of the hull outward) so that pegs with bundles of camouflage material may be fitted around the gunwale -- to hide both the punt and the occupant from the birds.
39. The coaming or splash rail fitted around the cockpit should not be glued to the boat. It should be bedded in a good seam compound and firmly screwed into place.

Also, since the coaming will be inside the camouflage, it could be made higher to add extra freeboard if very rough waters will be encountered.

40. Fiberglass the bottom and sides with a medium-weight glassing cloth and a self-curing resin. For best results follow the manufacturer's directions.
41. A ½" x 1" (1.27 x 2.5 cm) chine guard and two outer keels complete the wood work.
42. Fit those to the hull after the fiber glassing is complete and use seam/bedding compound before screwing to the hull.
43. The skegs or keels should be screwed right **through** the hull into the battens and frames **parallel** to the center line. Later they will help to protect the bottom from damage and keep the punt on a straight course when poling.

Woodworking Projects

44. Three coats of good marine enamel should cover the exposed wooden parts. For extra camouflage use any dull or flat finish paint and also spray with two or three additional colors over this. (Fiberglass can be covered with a good interior gel coat)
45. An extra ¾" plywood engine pad should be installed on the outside of the transom if an outboard is to be used. Its size is dictated by the transom and motor. (see plan)
46. To complement the punt, a combination pole-paddle should be made. It may resemble a long-handled canoe paddle; about 10 feet (3 m) long with a blade width of about 6 inches (15 cm). The blade tip should be bound in copper sheeting to prevent splitting. A straight-grained spruce plank is suitable for the job.
47. The single floorboard should fit loosely so that it can be removed without tools (rough 3/8" fir ply may be used to good advantage because **the floor should not ever be or become slippery**-- but you must treat it with a non-skid paint or when painting, sprinkle a handful of some dry sand on the wet paint.)

48. 5/16" plywood might require special framing joists to carry the operator's weight.
49. The recommended load limit is 350 pounds (175 kg). Outboard engine size should not exceed 3 horsepower.

P.S. The Marsh Fox can of course be built with other materials. For example, you can use fir plywood for the planking and decking. This will save time and money because you can then leave out the fiber glassing. Besides that, fir plywood is cheaper than mahogany but adds considerable weight to the punt.

N.B. Please do not use in big lakes or too far away from the shoreline. It is not designed for the high seas of the ocean. This punt is intended for sloughs and marshes. Be safe.

## OUTDOOR DECK (ADVANCE PLAN)

**Materials and Tools:**
- Sharp handsaw
- Claw hammer & heavy hammer
- Steel ruler
- Spirit level or equivalent laser bead
- String line
- Screwdrivers
- Wrench for 10mm or ½ inch bolts
- Spades, Picks & Shovels
- Builders Cement trowel

It would also be advisable to have these electrical tools to hand – hire them if necessary.
- Paslode nail gun or decking screw nail gun
- Chop-saw or bench saw
- Electric drill
- Cordless drill
- Electric jigsaw

On top of that you will need a selection of fittings such as these:
- Galvanized Nails for the Paslode (3in, 4in)
- Size 10 Galvanized coach bolts (7in, in)
- Joist strap hangers for 6x2 in timbers
- Long drill bit for coach bolts.

Materials for the job include:
- 6 x 2-inch treated timbers
- 4 x 4-inch treated posts
- Decking material
- Weed suppressant fabric material
- Sand and cement
- 7N dense concrete blocks
- Safety goggles and equipment

**Steps:**

STEP 1: Frame Construction

The frame that supports your deck, basically consists of 6 x 2 timbers bolted and nailed on to 4 x 4 posts on top of your concrete foundations. As mentioned earlier though, you may be able to use 4 x 2 timbers in some situations, but more support is required for stability.

Outdoor Deck (Advance Plan)

*Timber beams doubled up for extra strength. Crossbeams sitting on joint hangers.*

*Beams bolted to supporting posts with galvanized coach-bolts*

STEP 2: Laying Out the Levels

On most decking areas, especially when the deck is attached to a house, the levels are laid out from the house outward.

The first beam laid is running alongside the wall under the patio doors. Both the height of the 6 x 2 and the thickness of the decking timber has to be taken into account, in order to get the level correct when leaving the house.

This is sometimes determined by local building regulations, as some will insist on a 6 inch step down, where others are happy with just a slight drop when leaving the house.

Woodworking Projects

STEP 3: Laying the surface

This is in fact the easy part! First of all you must decide on whether to use screws or nails. The advantage in using screw nails is simply that you can unscrew them if things go bad. However it is a little slower using this method.

Galvanized nails from a Paslode nail gun or equivalent however is a very quick method of laying down the boards, but it is permanent, so if you make a mistake you will more than likely damage the boards while trying to lift them.

Outdoor Deck (Advance Plan)

STEP 4: Adding Handrails

Handrails are a necessary fitting to consider if you have any kind of a drop-away on your deck, or even just for aesthetic purposes.

In this example it is obvious that a protective handrail would need to be fitted, as the drop away on the stream side is over 30 feet!

These have to be securely bolted to the 6 x 2 frame-work, before the decking is laid, as this can be extremely difficult afterwards.

The railing sections themselves are better constructed in one piece and then fixed between the posts, as in this case. However there are many types of handrails that can be fitted to decking, and some of these are better fitted in situ between the posts. In this case I am using turned posts and spindles to create a safety handrail around the decking area.

Woodworking Projects

> 6 x 2 on edge, secured to deck, runs parallel to opposite framework
>
> Short lengths of 6 x 2 joins the step to the main deck.

STEP 5: Creating Steps

In any area where the ground is sloping, or indeed where you just want to break up the monotony of a large flat deck area; then you have to consider steps or raised platforms. There are a few ways you can do this (as usual) however in a sloping ground situation

STEP 6: Finishing the Deck

Outdoor Deck (Advance Plan)

The slabs themselves are simply laid on a dry mix of sand and cement (about 3-1) laid down, and then filled in with some ornamental pebbles from the garden center.

STEP 7: Treating Your Deck

Most decking material comes ready treated, indeed before building your frame-work in particular, you have to be sure that it is treated otherwise it will last no time at all, and a lot of hard work will be for nothing.

With hardwood decking, there is usually not much to do except re-treat with the necessary oils or specialist treatments, every couple of years or so after installation. With pressure injected softwood decking, then it is already treated for rot, and insects, so any treatment is just for aesthetic purposes really. If you do want to treat it to change the color for instance, then I would normally leave new decking for at least a couple of months so that it has time to dry out properly. The treatment process soaks the wood right through, so this is better dried out before you try and treat again.

Maintaining a deck after it is completed needn't be expensive or time consuming, certainly if you are not afraid of a little DIY. This is mainly a matter of keeping debris from building up, sanding down where needed, and treating every other year or so with a good quality wood stain or preservative.

**Slippery Deck Surface**
Decking can become extremely slippery after it has been down a while, when it becomes wet. This is caused by tiny algae that can grow on the surface that may not even be seen especially when dry. After a shower of rain however you have an instant skating rink! This can be a particular problem if the decking area is near or under overhanging tree branches, as the sap from the leaf's drips onto the deck.

Woodworking Projects

The answer to this is simple. Spray or brush in a suitable deck cleaner – that includes an algae killer and brush off with a stiff brush or preferably a power hose system.

This usually only has to be done once a year or so in order to stop the algae re-establishing itself.

# CONCLUSION

A woodworking novice or a beginner will make simple woodworking plans. Such plans give sufficient detail to make the wood project much easier to work. A great project to work in wood begins with a detailed plan. You can get work plans for wood from a lot of sources. Some of those plans would be better than others.

A beginner should always come up with an easy plan. If the plan isn't sufficiently detailed, they could get lost and quit. They could also make costly mistakes and cannot finish a project there. If a first woodwork project for beginners is a disappointment, they are doubtful to try again. Consider your first project a success, and use a simple plan for woodworking. With its precise specifications, they make woodworking more enjoyable and easier to read directions.

A good plan will have patterns of woodwork inside. Such designs are accurate to size and will save you money on materials. As material prices go up, a good plan that is easy to follow becomes more valuable. Easy woodworking plans limit or eliminate costly mistakes. Design is an essential part of a successful project for a beginner or a master woodworker.

A beginner woodworker needs a plan which goes into all aspects of the project in detail, from cutting the parts that are required to how they go together to the form of joints that are used to keep them together. From the collection of fasteners and adhesives, a simple approach should go into the precise detail that can be followed by the novice. Will it be nailed together or locked in?

As a beginner, you might even be able to buy wood that's already cut to size for a small extra cost. Purchasing timber cut to size allows you to build faster, and there's nothing more motivating than seeing your first woodworking project come together quickly.

First, it should give you a list of raw materials, timber types, and sizes. This will allow you to go out and buy the required timber from your local timber dealer.

Secondly, the woodworking plan should give you a list of the required hardware. This includes nail, screw, nut, and bolt types and sizes, as well as glue types and quantities.

Finally, the project plan should provide you with a set of instructions step by step. That's the actual value of a good plan. It will help you to advance your project through a step-by-step logical process, providing you with diagrams and close-ups all the way through.

You can build your project as quickly or as slowly as you like in this way, but knowing all the time that you are progressing in the right direction.

## Woodworking Projects

So if you're keen, excited, and ready to follow the instructions, you can build with wood in no time at all.

The first thing to consider when choosing woodworking plans is the design of the plan. A variety of woodwork projects have a variety of plans available, so whatever the project you are interested in, there is a woodwork plan that you can use for your project guidance.

Next is the complexity of the woodworking plans and whether you can follow the plan. It will probably be more comfortable, to begin with, basic woodwork plans if you start working on DIY woodwork, and working your way to more complex plans as you become more confident.

You will determine whether you have the resources to complete the tasks. If the tools are not available, you can buy them or borrow them from friends and family. You must also know how long you are prepared to invest in the project and be rational.

There are different artistic but straightforward woodwork plans available for beginners or for people who are not highly qualified.

Nonetheless, the most important thing is to get your hands-on good plans. The standard of the plans differentiates significantly in timber ventures. They should ideally come with easy to follow good illustrations and diagrams.

Good woodworking plans come with a list of materials, excellent descriptions, and explanations to help you follow the plan of your choice. Measurements are crucial for each part of the woodworking plan. If the measurements are wrong, this will only lead to time and money being wasted.

Among the initial obstacles a brand-new woodworker needs to get past is the worry of botching a job, and among the very best methods to deal with that apprehension is to merely "think outside the box." The majority of novices choose to begin with something easy (but might not know which projects have easy joinery), and after that, they set out on a hunt for preprinted plans to create such-and-such.

It can end up being aggravating if personal aid is not available. There are a number of methods to cure this, however here is one that has actually worked for numerous folks: forget other people's plans. Design what you require yourself. It isn't as difficult as one may believe, due to the fact that there is constantly some sort of restricting criteria to start with.

The point is, do not hesitate to start these projects by yourself. There is a huge knowledge base of woodworking insight available in print and online. If the undertaking does not end up as you'd intended, you can always start over, and you are going to have learned a lot along the way. We frequently discover more from our mistakes in working wood than from easy successes.

## Conclusion

Creating your own project can additionally imply adapting somebody else's plan to your own usage. It's rather typical for a woodworker to see the perfect blanket chest, couch table or display case, and after that, think "But I want mine to be ..." and revamp the whole structure. Do not hesitate to have faith your instincts and be imaginative when making a piece. Teach yourself; ask queries on online woodworking forums or at clubs and associations. You'll quickly astonish yourself with just how much you can do.

Woodworking Projects